The Beauty CON GAME

The Beauty CON GAME

by Umoja

TROJAN HORSE PRESS

First Edition
First Printing: March 2012

Library of Congress Control Number: 2012930393

ISBN: 9780982206133

Disclaimer for resemblance to real persons

This book includes political satire and works of fiction. Names, characters, places, and incidents are either the product of the authors' imaginations or used fictitiously. Any resemblance to actual persons, living or dead, business establishments, events, or locales is entirely coincidental. The publisher does not have any control over and does not assume any responsibility for any third-party websites or their content.

Printed and bound Manufactured in the United States of America

Trojan Horse Press
PO Box 245
Hazel Crest, IL 60429-1869

email: info@trojanhorse1.com
website: www.trojanhorse1.com

Cover Design by P. Evans

Dedication

To our beautiful black women, our mothers, wives, lovers, and best friends. To our strong, courageous black brothers, wherever you are, fighting for justice.

And a very special dedication to:

Dr. Frances Cress Welsing
Neely Fuller, Jr.
Gus Renegade
The Honorable Elijah Muhammad
Malcolm X
The Honorable Marcus Garvey

Acknowledgements

This book could not have been written or completed without the ground-breaking works of Neely Fuller, Jr., Dr. Frances Cress Welsing, the Honorable Elijah Muhammad, Haki R. Madhubuti, Dr. Yosef Ben-Jochannan, John Henrik Clarke, Marcus Garvey, Dr. Mwalimu K. Bomani Baruti, Chancellor Williams, Malcolm X, George Orwell, Tony Brown, Jawanza Kunjufu, Carter G. Woodson, James Baldwin, Willard Motley, and many others too numerous to mention. Naturally, we accept total responsibility for any misinterpretations of their works, and any errors that may appear in this book.

A very special thanks to Gus Renegade (C.O.W.S.), Sister Nefertari, H.H., D.H., Wendy Williams, R. Parker, J. Wickett, B. Harris, R., K. Richardson, D. Robinson, and of all our friends, family, and mentors who shared their special insights, wisdom, and patience with us.

We hope we have done some justice to all who inspired us to complete the second book in the Trojan Horse Trilogy, and that we have inspired others in the fight for universal justice for all the people on our Creator's planet.

About the Authors

Why the authors use a pseudonym

There is nothing original about the ideas presented here. Wiser minds have come before and will certainly come long after this book was written. The authors are not falsely modest; we are acknowledging we did not invent the wheel.

The authors are not seeking fame. This is not an attempt to be mysterious or provoke curiosity. This is not a gimmick or a perverse, reverse publicity ploy. In today's media-obsessed world, there is too much focus on "show" and not enough on "substance." The authors choose not to participate.

The authors reserve the right NOT to be a distraction to the message. We are the least important part of this book. You, the reader, are more important. Even more important, is what you do with this information.

Every word in this book was designed to inform, provoke discussion, decrease confusion, reduce hostility, minimize conflict, and to promote the kinds of constructive action that are necessary to replace the system of Racism/White Supremacy with a system of universal justice for **all the people on the planet.**

You may not agree with everything or anything written here. We have presented *our* truths to the best of our ability. If this book inspires you to seek your own truths, the book has been a success.

(The pseudonym, Anon for our first book, "Trojan Horse: Death Of A Dark Nation" has been replaced by "Umoja" - the Swahili word for "UNITY.")

Important Note To All Readers

Some chapters in our first three books -- 'Trojan Horse: Death of a Dark Nation,' 'Black Love Is A Revolutionary Act', and "The Interracial Con Game' -- have been included in our fourth book -- 'The Beauty Con Game' for the following reasons:

1. **NEW READERS** -- To get the most out of this book, it is important all readers understand what the Authors mean when we refer to the system of racism/white supremacy. It has been our experience that some readers are unaware that such a system exists OR that it controls every aspect of our lives as non-whites. Others may believe white supremacists represent a minority of poor whites -- the type that belongs to the Aryan Nation, the KKK, wear tattoos, or burn crosses. ***Nothing is further from the truth.***

2. **TO MAXIMIZE UNDERSTANDING** -- For many readers, the system of white supremacy is a NEW concept – but it is the MOST IMPORTANT concept that any black (or non-white) person will ever understand. Without that understanding, everything else you know will only confuse you. It is CRITICAL that our readers understand how the white supremacy system devastates the lives of black people, so we can make better decisions in RESPONSE to it.

3. **REPETITION IS THE KEY** -- to understanding AND remembering information. More repetition means MORE information will be ABSORBED and RETAINED.

4. **CONSISTENCY:** We felt it is important to be consistent from one book to the next, and the best way to do that was to provide the SAME explanations and definitions in all our books.

5. **HONESTY:** We felt it would be dishonest to rewrite the same chapters and pretend it was new information. We have included the table of contents of all our books on our website and on our Amazon.com pages so our readers will know exactly what they are getting in each book.

"Satoshi Kanazawa Causes Firestorm After Claiming Black Women Are Less Attractive"

-- referring to an article by Dr. Satoshi Kanazawa entitled, "Why are African-American women rated less attractive than other women?" in Psychology Today, May 15, 2011

The Purpose of this Book

The *"Beauty Con Game"* was originally written as a chapter in our first book, *"Trojan Horse: Death of a Dark Nation" by Anon* (our former pen name).

However, after the controversial article by Dr. Satoshi Kanazawa in May, 2011 (shown on the opposite page), we decided an entire book should be devoted to this topic because of the massive self-esteem damage that false beauty standards have wreaked among the black population.

As we researched this topic, we discovered that "beauty" -- or the so-called lack of it -- was used as a JUSTIFICATION to oppress blacks (and non-whites) *simply because they do not look like white people.* And we discovered something even more sinister:

Beauty had been 'scientifically" connected to intelligence and morality to DEVALUE non-white life and to justify the PAST, PRESENT, and FUTURE exploitation and extermination of millions of non-white people all over the planet.

The rise of racist black images in the media may be a response to the shrinking white populations all over the world. It is, therefore, DOUBLY important that black (and non-white) people understand there is much more at stake than whether whites think black people are "physically attractive."

The Authors will present the FACTUAL and HISTORICAL EVIDENCE that reveals how the second DEADLIEST CON GAME in human history -- the *BEAUTY CON GAME* -- threatens the survival of all non-white people -- and ULTIMATELY, of the planet itself.

That being said, this Book Was NOT Written to...

1. prove that blacks are as attractive as whites
2. make blacks feel superior to whites
3. convince whites that blacks are NOT inferior to whites
4. convince whites of anything regarding black people
5. degrade the physical features of any group of people
6. promote the mistreatment of any group of people

At the risk of offending some readers, we will NOT waste precious time being politically correct. We hope you will read this Book with an open and inquiring mind. Of course, the reader is free to agree or disagree with anything written here. Thank you for allowing us to share our insights and solutions) with you.

Contents

CHAPTERS

Why This Book Was Written

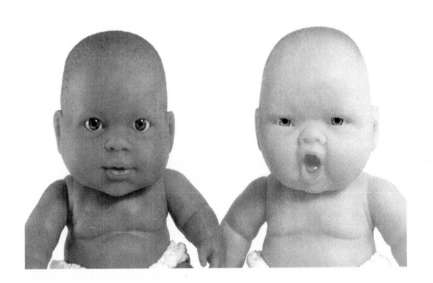

CHAPTER ONE

The Black Doll/White Doll Experiment

Two dolls, identical in appearance except for skin and hair color, were presented to a preschool-aged black girl. The female interviewer asked the little girl to choose the "bad doll." After her selection, the interviewer asked:

"And why does that look bad?"
"Because she's Black," the little girl answered.
"And why is this the nice doll?"
"Because she's White."
"And can you give me the doll that looks like you?"

After a slight hesitation, the little black girl picked up the black doll: *the bad doll.* Out of twenty-one black children tested, fifteen preferred the white doll over the black doll.

The More Things Change,
The More (Some) Things Stay The Same

This experiment -- conducted by a 16-year-old black female, Kiri Davis in 2006 -- was a duplicate of the original doll test by two black psychologists, Kenneth and Mamie Clark in 1954 (Clark's Black Doll/White Doll experiment). The married couple based the test on three studies they published on the effects of segregated schools on black children.

Kiri Davis's documentary, entitled, *A Girl Like Me* -- which she shot, edited and directed -- *over 50 years AFTER the Clark experiment* -- mirrored the same results.

While some have interpreted the low-self-esteem of black children as a byproduct of "segregated schools," *the Authors wholeheartedly DISAGREE.* It is NOT the lack of access to white children in a classroom that causes anti-blackness in black children; *it is the white supremacy system that teaches black inferiority/white superiority from cradle to grave.*

The Foundation For A 'Manufactured Black Inferiority Complex' Begins The Second A Black Child Sits In Front Of A TV Set

All children — regardless of ethnicity or economic class -- are born with a healthy amount of self-esteem. This does not change until something or someone says that child is NOT OK. Once a child is programmed to believe they are inferior, this creates a foundation for low self-esteem that will follow them into adulthood.

Some experts believe that a child's personality is formed by age three. For the black child, the outside world becomes an emotional landmine. All the things young children adore – children's TV shows, cartoons, movies, comics, popular toys, books, dolls, magicians, stuntmen, clowns, action heroes, Nancy Drew, the wildly popular Harry Potter, Disney characters, and a host of magical, mythical, and fantastic human beings – *show black children a wonderful world that is 99.99% WHITE.*

Even the most harmless household items, like "flesh-colored" crayons and Band-Aids become weapons of mass self-esteem destruction for black children. If they are old enough to understand that human beings are "flesh-colored," they might ask, "If human beings are pink, and my skin is brown, what does that make me?"

The recent trend over the last decade of mainly casting the so-called "bi-racial" child (a non-white child with a white parent) in TV commercials reinforces white superiority by making brown and dark-skinned children invisible (and inferior). It is common for television casting directors who hire a black boy or black girl in a TV commercial, to choose the non-white children of white females over brown and dark-skinned black children who look "too black."

By age four, black children have already internalized the white supremacy value system: *white is superior/black is inferior.* If a black child at that tender age already knows he or she is inferior to a white child, what happens to their self-esteem?

If a little black girl is brainwashed to believe the doll with the pale skin and blond hair is the prettiest BUT she is brown-skinned and dark-eyed, with a head full of soft, nappy hair, what does that do to her self-image, and later, her opinion of herself as a black woman?

How does the little black boy who picks the white doll as the "nicest" doll view (or value) his mother, sisters, aunts, and grandmothers if he is brainwashed to believe black females are inferior to white ones?

"I'm really not shocked, I am sad to say. Our children are bombarded with images every day...on television screens and on coffee tables— either the light-skinned female that everybody is pushing or they give preference to the closest to White images," says Julia Hare, a San Francisco psychologist. "Look at our rap artists and entertainers, and not just the Lil' Kims and the Beyoncés. Their skin is getting lighter and lighter and they're getting blonder and blonder."

Try to imagine white girls playing with nothing but black dolls and little white boys and girls seeing mostly positive images of blacks and mostly negative images of whites on TV? Now, try to imagine white parents sitting by silently and allowing this "damage" to happen to white children?

You can't imagine it because it would never happen.

Sanford And Son
"100 Best TV Shows Of All Time"
By Time Magazine (2007)

"I'm calling you ugly. I could push your face in some dough and make gorilla cookies."

Fred Sanford speaking to Aunt Esther, a dark-skinned black female. (from the hit TV series "Sanford and Son" (1972 -1977)

(Episodes of this "hit series" are running back to back on networks all over the country and have been viewed millions of times by three generations of black boys and girls)

Why Black Men Should Read This Book

"If I were white, I thought I could be a little happier. I wanted to be white because I was black, and black was never the right color."

-- Dennis Rodman, former NBA ballplayer, during an appearance on the Oprah Winfrey Show. He also revealed details about a 1993 suicide attempt, and that he didn't feel comfortable in the body he was given.

Sound-Off: Sammy Sosa's Pretty White Skin

"Sammy Sosa...his current conk, green contacts and continued use of skin lightening is a far departure from the Sammy Sosa of old -- a robustly brown-hued man with textured hair and dark eyes, i.e., he actually looked black."

-- Demetria L. Lucas, Essence Magazine, June 13th, 2011, speaking about Sammy Sosa, former pro baseball player

www.essence.com/2011/05/24/sammy-sosa-pretty-white-skin-bleaching-sound-off/

"Justice Clarence Thomas grew up in the 1950s. Due to having dark skin color, he was ridiculed by friends as "A.B.C.," an acronym meaning America's Blackest Child.

In the 1950s, prior to the "black is beautiful" movement, A.B.C. was the cruelest of names a black child could have. In addition, as the only black student enrolled in a Southern Catholic boarding school, Thomas was the daily butt of untold racist insults..."Smile, Clarence, so we can see you," a white classmate yelled after lights out.

Thomas has admitted to a period of self-hate in his life, which as a black conservative he projected onto other blacks as evidence of victim-group discrimination."

-- 'An Historical Analysis of Skin Color Discrimination' by Ronald E. Hall

"'Yes, it does have to be real hair. I want my kids to have nice hair so she better have good hair.

Cause, I don't know if you've checked my hair out lately. Aside from today it's normally nice. Today it's slightly nappy."

-- Actor Isaiah Mustafa (featured in Old Spice commercials), during a September 2011 "E! News" interview, told host Guiliana Rancic that his own hair was too "nappy."

Michael Jackson Had Dozens Of Skin-Whitening Creams: Documents

"Detectives found large quantities of general anesthetic and dozens of tubes of skin-whitening creams in Michael Jackson's home after the singer's death, search warrants unsealed Friday show."

-- AP entertainment writer, Anthony McCartney (March 26, 2010)

(www.huffingtonpost.com/2010/03/26/michael-jackson0had-dozen_n_515528.html)

"I was shocked to learn that the dancehall artist Vybz Kartel...is launching a range of cosmetics this month including his own brand of skin lightener.

It's something of a (un)natural progression from the (black) musician's decision earlier to lighten his own skin and the launch of his own "cake soap," a traditional Jamaican product intended for white clothes but which is reportedly misused to alter skin colour."

-- posted by LanréBakare (Sept 2011)

www.guardian.co.uk/fashion/fashion-blog/2011/sep/07/skin-bleaching-whitening-vybz-kartel

Taye Diggs: "Tyson Beckford Helped Me Like My Skin Color"

"Taye Diggs...says that he did not accept his skin color until he saw model Tyson Beckford's rise to fame. The actor/author says that he did not think he was good-looking at first because he had a complex about his skin color." (Jan 2012)

http://hellobeautiful.com/gossip-news/hellobeautiful-staff1/taye-diggs-tyson-beckford-helped-me-like-my-skin-color/?omcamp=EMC-CVNL

Taye Diggs Admits "My Mother Always Knew I'd Marry A White Girl!"

"My mother said 'I told you!" [laughs]. She always thought – I hate this, but I'm being honest! [laughs] – she said, "I always knew you were gonna marry a white girl!" The actor appeared on Sway's morning satellite radio show in 2011 to promote his new children's book (about loving dark skin?)

http://hellobeautiful.com/gossip-news/hellobeautiful-staff2/taye-diggs-wife-idina-menzel-sway-interview-mother-marry-white-girl/

CHAPTER TWO

FOUR Reasons Black Males Should Read A Book About Beauty

REASON #1 – Black Males Who Despise The Person In Their Mirrors

From cradle to grave, blacks are bombarded with negative messages about brown and dark skin, African features, and kinky hair. The darker-skinned we are, the more we are degraded and mistreated.

Black males are just as conflicted over skin color, hair, and facial features as black females, but it is not as obvious because males are not pressured to transform their faces, hair, and bodies with makeup, hair straighteners, weaves, and plastic surgery to look more "attractive" by white standards. However, the increase in black males having plastic surgery and using skin lighteners tells a different story.

While the 'Beauty Con Game' is more lethal for females than it is for males, being black and male in a black-male-hating society can wreak the kind of massive self-esteem devastation seen by the examples on the previous pages.

For millions of black males, the little black boy (inside) is STILL picking the white doll as the "best doll."

REASON #2 – Racist Images of Black Males In The Media

Black men are more likely to be seen wearing handcuffs than a tailored suit or doctor's scrubs. Black males cuffed in the back of a squad car; riddled with bullets on a city street; rotting in a jail cell; or lying on a cold slab in the county morgue scarcely raises an eyebrow or our blood pressure anymore.

Most movies and TV shows aimed at black youth depict black males as thugs, pimps, drug dealers, hustlers, poor, criminals, deadbeat baby daddies, clowns, court jesters, rapists, athletes, entertainers, buffoons, fools, and animalistic brutes. Dark-skinned black males are synonomous with low intelligence, criminality, and sexual predators. The darker they are, the more demonized AND victimized by white society they will be.

Even money and fame offer little protection for rich and/or famous dark-skinned black males, like Wesley Snipes and Michael Vick, who were sent to prison for minor offenses. This sends a powerful message to black male youth, making them doubt their OWN humanity and self-worth:

"I thank god that I am not basic
I am not a human being."
(lyrics from Lil' Wayne's song "I'm Not Human")

Regardless of the obvious financial reasons black rappers like Lil' Wayne promote the kind of "music" and lyrics that degrades black people, it is extremely DANGEROUS for black males to devalue their OWN BLACK LIVES in a black-male-hating society, especially when they are promoted by white media as the biggest role models for black youth.

Reason #3 – The Rising Number Of Black Males Who Are Committing Genetic Suicide

Some black males are so repelled by the image in their own mirrors, that they are deliberately breeding with white, Asian, or Hispanic females to rid their offspring of the racial 'ugliness' they secretly (and sometimes openly) believe exists within themselves (see page 13).

REASON #4 – Degrading the Beauty of Our Black Mothers Degrades ALL Black Life -- Male AND Female

"The "social position" of a race is determined by the social position of the female." - Karl Marx. In EVERY culture *the mother is sacred*; the "civilizer" of her culture, community, children, and society.

The black female is the CREATOR of all authentically black life. She is the FIRST TEACHER and her primary responsibility is to "civilize" the children by passing along the values and traditions of her culture to the next generation. The way the female sees herself will determine the way her offspring ultimately SEES, VALUES, and RESPECTS THEMSELVES.

When the white media degrades the black female's physical features and moral character, they are DELIBERATELY devastating the self-esteem of the products of her WOMB: *little black girls and boys who will one day grow up to be low-self-esteemed black men and women.*

If the "Mother" of a nation is a worthless whore how can the products of her womb (her children) have any value?

Once the BLACK MOTHER (the black female) is so degraded and demoralized that she becomes "uncivilized," she will not be able to civilize anyone else. As a result, her children, her men, her community, and the ENTIRE BLACK NATION will become demoralized, self-hating, self-disrespecting, and UNCIVILIZED. This lays the foundation for a 'Manufactured Black Inferiority Complex' that will last a lifetime.

Until blacks collectively understand the importance of protecting the IMAGE of the Black Mother of our Black Nation, we will continue reaping one damaged black generation after another.

A scene from the movie 'Birth of a Nation' (1915)

The movie, directed by D.W. Griffith, premiered with the title, 'The Clansman,' and was the highest-grossing film of the silent-picture era. The controversial and inflammatory film portrayed the Ku Klux Klan as heroes, and protectors of (pure) "white womanhood,"and portrayed black males as animalistic savage brutes who raped white females.

"When you teach a man to hate his lips, the lips that God gave him, the shape of the nose that God gave him, the texture of the hair that God gave him, the color of the skin that God gave him, you've committed the worst crime that a race of people can commit." -- Malcolm X (1925 - 1965)

Why Black Females Are The Main Focus Of This Book

"She looks like a ghetto slut...her new hair-do makes her look like...an explosion at a Brillo pad factory...like Tina Turner peeing on an electric fence."

-- Neal Boortz, a white male, referring to black congresswoman, Rep. Cynthia McKinney (D-GA) -- the first black woman elected to Congress from Georgia -- on a broadcast of his nationally syndicated radio program (March 31, 2006).

On August 9, 2006, the MTV network broadcast a new cartoon portraying two bikini-wearing black women, squatting on all fours, with leashes around their necks, and defecating (using the bathroom) on the floor.

Supposedly, the show was lampooning Snoop Dogg, who had no involvement in the show.

The show aired at 12:30 pm on Saturday when thousands of children, teens, and young adults were watching.

The cable TV station, owned by Viacom, Inc., a media giant, defended the episode, by calling it "social satire."

"I would have to say that Haitian hookers are probably infected with a whole bunch of stuff, you might have to...you know what? Maybe this is actually a good thing."

'Bubba the Love Sponge,' a white male Florida "shock jock," referring to the 7.0 Magnitude earthquake in Haiti in 2010 where over 200,000 (black) men, women, and children were feared dead. 'Bubba' was NOT fired for making the comment.

Radio Talk Show Host Fired For Racial Slur Against Condoleeza Rice

"She's been chancellor of Stanford. She's got the patent resume of somebody that has serious skill. She loves football. She's African-American, which would kind of be a big coon. A big coon. Oh my God. I am totally, totally, totally, totally, totally sorry about that."

St. Louis radio talk show host, Dave Lenihan, white male, referring to the first black female Secretary of State, Condolezza Rice

(Source: www.foxnews.com March, 2006)

(A month later, Dave Lenihan was back on the air at the same radio station. Station owner, Dennis Klautzer, said, "I consider him a great talent...It was obviously a slip of the tongue."

Howard Stern: Gabourey Sidibe Is 'Enormous,' Will Never Work Again

"There's the most enormous, fat black chick I've ever seen. She is enormous. Everyone's pretending she's a part of show business and she's never going to be in another movie...Oprah's another liar, a filthy liar. She's telling an enormous woman the size of a planet that she's going to have a career."

-- Howard Stern, white male, on his Sirrus satellite show, March 2010.
     Source: www.huffingtonpost.com)

"Take that bone out of your nose and call me back." -- Rush Limbaugh, talk show host, to black female caller.

***

"...It doesn't look like Michelle Obama follows her own nutritionary advice...I'm trying to say that our First Lady does not project the image of women you might see on the cover of Sports Illustrated Swimsuit Issue or of a woman Alex Rodriguez might date every six months or what have you."
      -- Rush Limbaugh, talk show host
         (Source: www.alan.com)

RACISM = MILLIONS OF WHITE FANS AND MILLION-DOLLAR PAYDAYS
For White Talk-Radio/TV 'Shock Jocks'

- Howard Stern, rated the most highly paid, high-profile talk host in the business by Talkers Magazine, reportedly makes $100 million a year.

- Rush Limbaugh, America's most widely listened to talk-radio host, signed an eight-yr, $300 million contract extension with Clear Channel in August 2008 worth $37.5 million a year.

- 'Bubba the Love Sponge' reportedly makes $1 million a year and has satellite radio's second-largest audience.

- Don Imus signed a 5-year deal with Citadel that pays him between $5 and $8 million annually and is heard on more than 80 stations nationwide.

- Neal Boortz reportedly makes $200,000 a year, is allegedly American's most popular 'Libertarian' talk-show host, and was rated one of the top 25 Most Influential Talk Radio Hosts in America by Newsmax.com

- In 2004, while interviewed by Alan Colmes, Opie and Anthony allegedly agreed they were paid $3 Million per year. In October, 2011, their show's station was changed to 'The Opie and Anthony Channel.'

"That's some rough girls from Rutgers. Man, they...some hard-core hos. That's some nappy-headed hos there."

-- Don Imus, white male shock jock, "joking" about the black teenaged girls on the Rutgers basketball team (April 7, 2007). Imus was fired shortly after the incident AND rehired:

"Citadel Broadcasting Corporation and 77 WABC Radio announced today the return of radio's lone cowboy Don Imus as the station's new morning host beginning Monday, Dec. 3. Imus signed a 5-year deal with Citadel that pays him between $5 and $8 million annually.

"We are ecstatic to bring Don Imus back to morning radio," said 77 WABC President and General Manager Steve Borneman."

CHAPTER THREE

Black Females Are The Main Targets Of "Beauty" Terrorism

Since BEAUTY is largely a feminine concept, females are more likely than males to be JUDGED, VALUED, and DEVALUED solely by how far they rate up or down on the "attractiveness" scale. Men are also victimized by beauty standards but are able to overcome their physical shortcomings by bringing money, status, power, and/or fame to the table.

In a white supremacy society (like America) whites set the standard for what is "normal" and good. "Whiteness" is given the highest value, and the "whitest" female with the palest skin, hair, and eyes is placed at the top of the beauty totem pole, while the "blackest" female with the darkest skin, hair, and eyes is forced to the bottom.

When it comes to BEAUTY, all non-white females – black, red, brown, and yellow – are INFERIORIZED (made to appear inferior) to maintain the superior position of the white female.

BEAUTY then becomes **a zero-sum equation:** *if one thing is good; the opposite must be bad. In other words, for the white female to be beautiful (good), the black female must be ugly (bad).*

While it's true that black males are severely degraded in the mainstream media – especially dark-skinned black males – their degradation has more to do with stereotyping their behavior rather than ridiculing their physical features. **The proof:**

Black males are NOT pressured to look "whiter" or to have longer, straighter, processed, or weaved hair -- *or any hair at all.* Black male sex symbols range from the darkest complexions (like Wesley Snipes) to the lightest complexions (like Boris Kodjoe) BUT it is **difficult to impossible** to name ONE black actress as DARK-SKINNED as Samuel Jackson who plays the role of a desirable sex symbol in ANY Hollywood-produced movie or TV show, OR in ANY independent black film for that matter.

Black females are the MOST likely group in America to be *targeted AND terrorized* by the (white) mainstream media and by white society in general *based SOLELY on the way they look.* For example, in the May 2011 issue of Psychology Today:'

"Why are African-American Women Rated Less Attractive Than Other Women, But Black Men Are Rated Better Looking Than Other Men?"

To understand HOW *'The Beauty Con Game'* threatens the survival of ALL black people everywhere on the planet, let's start where it all began: *at the beginning...*

The Deadliest Con Game:

Racism/White Supremacy

"...and the People of the River are black people, and the
People of the Plains are brown people, and the People
of the Mountains are red people, and the People of the
Forest are yellow people..."

CHAPTER FOUR

A WHITE SUPREMACY "FAIRY TALE"

(TRUTH IS STRANGER THAN FICTION)

Excerpted from an article
by Edward Williams
(www.counter-racism.com)

Looking at how the universe works...we are all people. All of the people in the known universe are only people. Picture that in your mind. Now some people come in contact with other people and say that they are white people.

And you say "OK" because you don't know what they are talking about. Now just because they say they are "white people" instead of calling themselves "people" means they have an agenda.

Wherever you are on the planet the people are identified by where they are located. People of the River, People of the Plains, People of the Mountains, People of the Forest and they may or may not have one word to describe it. Such as the Paoli people where Paoli means "People of the River."

Now...in addition to saying they are white people they also say that you are a non-white person. And you say, "OK" because you still don't know where they are going with all of this. Now... they also say that the People of the River, People of the Plains, People of the Mountains and the People of the Forest are also non-white people.

The white people say that the People of the River are black people, and that the People of the Plains are brown people, and the People of the Mountains are red people, and the People of the Forest are yellow people.

Everyone says "OK" because they still don't know where these people who say that they are "white people" are going with all of this. And over the years the people really buy into the idea of being black or brown or red or yellow...so much so that they begin to become proud of being black or brown or red or yellow and shout each other down about it while the white people are just watching them shout each other down about it.

One day a child comes along and asks, to a white person, *"Why do you say I'm a black person?"* And the white person, while laying on their death bed says, *"It means that you do what I tell you to do and if you don't do it I will shoot you."*

That is what racism (white supremacy) is all about. It means that every person who is not white (non-white) qualifies for mistreatment based on that alone. You don't qualify for mistreatment based on what you do or don't do or because of what you may say or not say.

You are qualified for mistreatment because you are not a white person. Just because you are not a white person. And there are many words or terms that are used to describe the people who are non-white such as:

- colored people
- negroes
- chinks
- niggers
- sand niggers
- spics
- darkies
- black people
- red people
- yellow people
- brown people
- slant-eyed
- darkie
- tribe
- natives
- indians

...and the list goes on and on.

We -- meaning all non-white people -- are just a group of people who are victims of racism (white supremacy). It is time we understand how the white people who practice racism (white supremacy) are the smartest, most powerful white people, and how they view the world, and how they manage people based on their world view. We have to begin to talk like we understand what they are doing.

When someone asks me if I am a black person, I usually say "I am a person who is a victim of racism (white supremacy). I have been known to say that I am a black person and when I do say I am a black person I simply mean that I understand that I have been targeted for mistreatment because I have been identified, by white people, as not being a white person.

Just like the People of the River, People of the Plains, People of the Mountains, and the People of the Forest...targeted for mistreatment.

The End

"The only reason white people would want their "genes" to survive is so that they could survive as "white people," and the only reason they would want to survive as white people would be to practice white supremacy (racism).

It has been my observation that white people do not want to survive as white people for the sake of surviving as white people...it is for the sake of being in the powerful position over the other people on the planet.

In other words, being a white person has no value and no function except in the SYSTEM of white supremacy (racism)."

-- Edward Williams
(www.counter-racism.com)

"If you do not understand White Supremacy (Racism), what it is, and how it works, everything else that you understand, will only confuse you."

Neely Fuller, Jr. (1971)

CHAPTER FIVE

WHAT IS RACISM/WHITE SUPREMACY?

"Racism is white supremacy. White supremacy is racism. There is no other form." -- Neely Fuller, Jr.

Let's Begin At The Beginning By Defining The Words:

1. **White Supremacy** -- a social, economic, and political system based on the belief that whites are superior to non-whites. (the Foundation).
2. **Racism** -- the systematic discrimination (the denial of rights and benefits) by whites against non-whites in all areas of human activity: (1) economics, (2) education, (3) entertainment, (4) labor, (5) law, (6) politics, (7) religion, (8) sex, and (9) war. (the Behavior). *Racism = Power + Prejudice.*

Q: Why is it called "Racism/White Supremacy?"
A: Because this describes exactly WHO is practicing racism. For one group to practice racism that group must have MORE POWER than another group. Since whites control **ALL** the major areas of human activity in America -- housing, education, health, entertainment, economics, politics, law, and religion -- it is accurate to define all "**racism**" as "**white supremacy.**" We must be accurate so the victims of racism do not become confused.

Q: Isn't all racism the same, regardless of who is practicing it?
A: There is only ONE kind of racism: **white supremacy**. White people are the only group in America with the POWER to discriminate (deprive or punish other ethnic groups), and the systems and institutions to maintain the imbalance of power.

For example, rich people are more powerful than poor people. Rich people have the POWER to discriminate against poor people by depriving them of income, promotions, jobs, housing, land, and any other rights – if they choose to do so. Racism is not empty rhetoric (words) or mindless emotion. Racism is social, economic, and political POWER.

In America, whites have the POWER to discriminate against blacks (and other non-whites) by depriving them of income, promotions, jobs, housing, land, justice, and any other rights – if they choose to do so. It doesn't matter that some whites are poorer than some blacks.

In all things and in all places in America, whites are **collectively** more powerful than blacks are **collectively**. This imbalance of (white) power creates the opportunity and the ability to practice racism against non-whites.

Q: Why do you refer to non-whites as "groups" instead of "races?"
A: Because there is ONLY ONE RACE: *the white race.* To prove this statement, let's look at the TRUE meaning of "race." In ancient civilizations tens of thousands of years ago (before Europeans inhabited the planet), the world's people identified themselves by bloodline, birthplace, and culture – but NEVER by the artificial construct (concept) of "race."

What is the "black race" in real terms? It does NOT describe the place where black people were born because there is no such place as "black land," (or red, yellow, brown, or white land). Race does not describe a person's religion because there is no such thing as a black, red, brown, yellow, or white religion.

Race does not describe a person's culture (except in false, stereotypical terms), and it does NOT define biology, ethnicity, or nationality. Race does not describe skin color because the so-called "black race" includes people whose complexions range from the palest pink to the purest blue-black. *Therefore, "race" is a false, manmade concept.*

Q: If "race" is a false concept, why was it created?
A: Race was created for ONLY one purpose: *to practice race-ism (racism).* To practice "racism," whites had to separate themselves from other groups of people by artificially creating different "races."

Q: Why was "racism/white supremacy" created?
A: Dr. Frances Cress Welsing, a black psychiatrist and the author of *'The Isis Papers: The Keys to the Colors'* (1991), states that White Supremacy is practiced by the global "white" minority on the conscious and unconscious level to ensure their genetic survival by any means necessary.

Because of their "numerical inadequacy," whites may have defensively developed *"an uncontrollable sense of hostility and aggression" towards people of color, and developed a social, political, and economic structure to give blacks and other 'non-whites' the appearance of being inferior."*

The Authors will add one more reason: Racism/white supremacy was created to allow the people who classify themselves as "white" to economically, socially, politically, sexually, psychologically, and genetically DOMINATE all the people who they classify as "non-white."

Q: Who decides what "race" a person will be?
A: The same (white) people who created the concept of race. If the ONLY purpose of "race" is to practice racism, and whites are the only group or "race" (in a white supremacy system) that can practice racism, then it is logical to assume there is ONLY ONE RACE: *the white race.*

Q: If the white race is the only race, what are the other 'groups' called?
A: There are three types of people in a white supremacist system:

1. Non-white people
2. White people (Racist Suspects)
3. White Supremacists (Racists)

Q: What is a "Non-White" person?
A: Anyone who is NOT classified as "white." This includes all black, red, yellow, and brown people aka "people of color."

Q: What is a "Racist Suspect?"
A: ANY white person who is CAPABLE of practicing racism against non-whites. Since all whites are able to practice racism in a white supremacy system if they choose to do so, it is correct (and logical) to use the term "racist suspects" to identify whites who do not openly function as white supremacists (racists). This is not a hateful, unjust, or racist statement, but it is a **logical statement**.

Q: What is a "White Supremacist?"
A: A white person (a racist) who practices racism against non-whites. Being a white supremacist has nothing to do with income, title, or status. It does not mean a white person belongs to the KKK, the Aryan Nation, or is covered with Nazi tattoos.

A white supremacist can be a soccer mom, a businessman, or a US Senator if they are practicing racism against non-whites. Another term for a white supremacist is "racist man" and "racist woman."

Q: How can a non-white person determine if a white person is a racist?
A: Non-whites cannot always determine who is a racist, and who is not, because it is impossible to monitor (or judge) all the individual actions and words of any white person at all times. To illustrate this point:

Case Of The Stolen Wallet

There are five people in a room when a wallet that belongs to a sixth person (who is not in the room) is stolen. All five are "suspects" because every person in the room had the ability and the opportunity to take the wallet. This does not mean all five are thieves NOR does it mean all five are not thieves, because any of them could have stolen something at an earlier time.

As it turns out, two of the five people in the room CONSPIRED to steal the wallet by breaking into the sixth person's locker. The other three saw it happen, did not participate in the crime, did not care that the wallet was stolen, and did and said nothing to stop it from happening.

The sixth person – the owner of the wallet -- has no idea who stole it, if anyone saw what happened, or how many participated in the theft. All he knows is has been the VICTIM of a crime because his wallet is missing.

The two people who stole the wallet are guilty of "commission" – they actually **committed the crime**. The three witnesses are guilty of "omission" since they **witnessed the crime, said nothing and did nothing to stop it, and refused to help the victim with the information they had.**

The next day the two thieves treat the three witnesses to lunch, paying for it with the money from the stolen wallet. The witnesses did not steal the wallet but are knowingly or unknowingly benefiting from the theft. The three witnesses are not **legally liable**, but they are **morally liable,** and are correctly viewed as **"suspects" by the victim.**

Racism operates the same way. There are whites who:

- are practicing racism against non-whites at a particular moment
- are not practicing racism at that moment but have practiced it at a previous time, or will practice it at a later time
- are not practicing racism at that moment, but say and do nothing to stop those who are
- are not practicing racism at that moment, but have no problem with other whites practicing racism (don't care)
- are benefiting from the crime of racism even if they are not practicing racism at that moment
- refuse to tell WHO is practicing racism; HOW racism is being practiced; and refuse to help the victims with the information they have
- oppose racism by exposing and opposing whites who practice it

Another Example:

Mr. X, a black management trainee, is looking for an apartment closer to his new job. He calls an upscale rental complex near his office, and asks if they have any one-bedroom apartments.

The rental agent, a young white male, says there are two one-bedroom apartments available, takes Mr. X's name and phone number, and asks him to stop by and fill out an application.

The next day Mr. X stops by the complex after work. A different rental agent, Mrs. W, a middle-aged white female, greets him in the reception area. She says she's sorry, but there are no apartments available.

She suggests he fill out an application so they will have his information on file, and assures Mr. X that he will be the first one she calls when a one-bedroom becomes available.

Mr. X is immediately suspicious, but he fills out an application anyway. On his way home, he replays the conversation with the rental agent. Mr. X has no way of knowing if the first rental agent made an honest mistake, or if he has just been a victim of racial discrimination. His gut tells him it was the latter.

The Crime

When Mrs. W saw Mr. X was black, she used the same line she always used with black applicants. Later, she warns the new rental agent -- who talked to Mr. X over the phone – to never rent to blacks or Hispanics.

The Victim

Like the man whose wallet was stolen, Mr. X is the victim of a crime. The problem is, Mr. X can't be sure a crime was even committed, which makes it more difficult for him to protect himself from being victimized in the future. It is this kind of confusion that wreaks the most psychological damage on black people who run a DAILY risk of being victimized by racism – without being able to prove they were victimized.

The Criminals

Mrs. W is guilty of commission (practicing racism). The new rental agent is guilty of omission because he said and did nothing, and refused to help Mr. X with the information he had (that another white person, Mrs. W, was practicing racism).

It is the *crime of commission AND omission* that allows the system of racism/white supremacy to function so effectively. The system does not require all whites to practice racism at all times, but it does require that **the majority of whites say and do nothing when racism is occurring and allow themselves to benefit from the victimization of non-whites.**

Those benefits include better jobs, housing, food, medical care, education, police protection, justice, etc., than non-whites. If the majority of whites were opposed to racism/white supremacy, it would NOT be the most powerful social, economic, and political system on the planet.

It is LOGICAL to assume that the majority (or possibly all) white people have made a DELIBERATE DECISION to do one or all of the following:

- practice racism
- do nothing and say nothing to stop others from practicing racism
- deny racism is being practiced even when they know it is happening
- refuse to help the victims of racism with the information they have

That's why simple-minded thinking is useless when determining which white person is a racist and which one is not. It cannot be determined by a white person's sexual behavior. White slave owners had sexual relations with male and female slaves but they were still white supremacists (racists).

Whites have engaged in sexual relations with black people, but that doesn't mean they are not racists. Whites who have black friends, wives, husbands, or children are still "racist" if they are practicing racism against non-whites. It cannot be determined by observing the words or the actions of a particular white person, who may or may not be practicing racism at that particular time.

It cannot be determined by a random (or deliberate) act or acts of kindness toward a non-white person. Mass child-murderer John Gacy was "kind" to children when he performed in his clown costume. There were slave-owners who were "kind" to their slaves, but not kind enough to stop selling human beings.

AXIOM #1: YOU CANNOT OPPOSE SOMETHING AND KNOWINGLY BENEFIT FROM IT AT THE SAME TIME.

It is LOGICAL in a white supremacist society to assume the **majority of whites** are either practicing racism (the act of commission), or are cooperating with those who are, by saying and doing nothing to stop them, refusing to help the victims of racism with the information they have (the act of omission), and are *benefiting* from the practice of racism.

Q: Do non-racist whites benefit from White Supremacy?

A: ALL whites benefit from white privilege in a white supremacy system, even if they are not practicing racism at that moment. It does not matter if they are rich or poor; or whether they admit there is such a thing as white privilege. Anyone who is classified as "white" in a white supremacy system will always have advantages over someone who is not. Just as a black person in a black supremacy system (if one existed) would have advantages over someone who is not black.

Q: Aren't some white people opposed to racism?

A: Only if they are saying and doing something to oppose it. For example, John Brown, a white male, encouraged armed insurrection by slaves as a means to end slavery, and as a result, was charged with treason and hanged. However, that does not mean John Brown did not practice racism at an earlier time OR would not have practiced it at a later time had he lived.

Q: Aren't white anti-racists opposed to racism?

The self-annointed, white anti-racist activist offers little more than LIP SERVICE. They sacrifice NOTHING, take NO risks, and reap MORE financial rewards than the black activists fighting in the (real) trenches.

The white anti-racist actually creates MORE confusion by creating the FALSE illusion that the devastated black masses can be liberated from racism by sitting in a church, auditorium, or conference room listening to a white person -- who is STILL enjoying his or her white privileges -- making anti-racism speeches.

It is UNLIKELY that the same white anti-racist activists who PROFIT from writing books and giving speeches about racism -- have any real desire (or intent) to destroy the same white supremacy system that allows them to oppose it without losing a single 'white privilege.'

There may be whites who are sincere about replacing the system of white supremacy with a system of justice, *but that number is so statistically small, it is insignificant.*

Q: When a black person mistreats a white person, isn't that "racism/black supremacy?"

A: No, because black supremacy does not exist. If black people were collectively more powerful than whites collectively, blacks would have the power to practice racism. Logically speaking, that would mean the end of white supremacy.

AXIOM #2: BLACK SUPREMACY CAN EXIST ONLY IN THE TOTAL ABSENCE OF WHITE SUPREMACY. WHITE SUPREMACY CAN EXIST ONLY IN THE TOTAL ABSENCE OF BLACK SUPREMACY. THE TEXTBOOK DEFINITION OF "SUPREMACY" IS:

THE HIGHEST RANK OR AUTHORITY.

THIS MEANS ONLY ONE THING CAN BE "SUPREME" OR OCCUPY THE "HIGHEST RANK" AT A TIME.

If blacks and whites had equal power and resources, there could be no black supremacy OR white supremacy. Our ability (power) to discriminate against (mistreat) each other would be cancelled out, leaving only two options: *coexist peacefully or destroy each other.*

A Question From A Reader On The Meaning Of "Race"

"In your second book, 'Black Love Is A Revolutionary Act,' pg.130, I understand "race" is a false concept, and why it was created, to be able to group and classify non-white people for the purpose of practicing racism.

I agree race does not describe culture, biology, ethnicity, or nationality. Race does not describe skin color because the so-called "black race" includes complexions from pale to blue-black. My question is how is the white race the only race? If white racists created the concept, can they create reality?" – Thomas D.

ANSWER: That's a good question, Thomas. The first time we heard Mr. Neely Fuller, Jr. say there was only one race -- the white race -- this was confusig because it went against EVERYTHING we had been taught about the word, "race." However, once we followed the LOGIC, we realized Mr. Fuller was correct.

If **"race"** was created for ONLY one purpose -- to practice **"race-ism"** (racism) -- AND white people are the ONLY people who have the POWER to practice **"racism,"** it is LOGICAL to conclude that *the only race is the white race.*

Can the white supremacists create reality? Think of the white supremacy system as a **MATRIX** created by the smartest, most powerful white people on the planet to control all the non-white people.

Before white people came into existence, the non-white people made up names for themselves but after white people started oppressing non-whites all over the world, white people RE-NAMED all the non-white people and all the places they came from.

The non-white people DID NOT UNDERSTAND that white people were setting up a SYSTEM that would allow them to mistreat non-white people *on the basis of color*, so the non-white people went along with it.

COMMON SENSE tells us that the "black race" CANNOT be an accurate description of a people who number in the BILLIONS; who come from all over the world; who have different cultural practices and backgrounds; who speak different languages; who practice different religions; who eat different foods; and have all types of skin tones, hair textures, and facial features. There is one even more compelling reason:

If black people (Africans) were the first people on earth -- and even the smartest white people on the planet say this is true -- then EVERY man, woman, and child on earth DESCENDED from the "black race" -- including white people!

That being said, even though a *"black race"* is a false concept, the Authors still refer to ourselves as *"black people"* for the following reasons:

1. We are **black people** because **people exist** -- BUT we cannot be part of a (nonexistent) "black race" because there is ONLY one race: *the white race.*

2. We have been classified as **"black people"** by the white supremacists who dominate all black and non-white people under the system of white supremacy.

3. We have been targeted for mistreatment as **black people -- and our mistreatment is a reality.**

4. We are spiritually, historically, genetically, culturally, biologically, emotionally, sexually, and romantically CONNECTED to the people that the white supremacists have classified as *"black people."*

We hope we've answered your questions. We recommend you review the previous chapters on Racism/White Supremacy (pp 37-43) until the concept becomes a natural part of your foundation.

We also recommend that you listen to the interviews of Mr. Neely Fuller Jr. with Gus Renegade on the C.O.W.S. (Context Of White Supremacy) -- www.contextofwhitesupremacy.com and visit www.counter-racism.com

The Authors

The
Beauty
Con
Game

"Once you convince someone to hate the reflection in their mirror, you can convince them of anything."

Umoja

CHAPTER SIX

DEBUNKING THE TOP TEN
BEAUTY CON GAME MYTHS

The old cliché -- "Beauty's in the eye of the beholder" – is no match for the power of white supremacy. Under this system, beauty has become a zero-sum equation for whites and non-whites, which states: (1) If whites are the most attractive, non-whites must be the least attractive. (2) If light skin is a sign of (racial) beauty, dark skin must be a sign of (racial) ugliness.

Black Inferiority Complexes Are Rooted In Our Mirrors

This (false) man-made concept of beauty is used to instill the FIRST seeds of self-hatred and inferiority in non-white children -- in particular, in the darkest-skinned people. It is critical that we understand how the **Beauty Con Game** functions so we will understand why so many non-whites despise the person in their mirrors.

MYTH #1: We Should Take Credit For An Accident Of Birth

We have no control over the parents we have, the genes we inherit, or the color of the woman that delivered us into this world. Giving ourselves credit for being born white, black, red, or green; light or dark-skinned; six-foot-two or four-foot-one; blue-eyed or brown-eyed; is the same as taking credit for having two hands and two feet.

Our skin color is an accident of birth; a random toss of the genetic dice. To base our superiority on something we had no control over is foolish. We should only take credit for what we have personally accomplished.

MYTH #2: God Made Whites Superior To Blacks

If this is true then the following must also be true:

1. God CANNOT be all-powerful and all-knowing because He made the African man and woman the first people on earth. (He made a mistake).

2. Two inferior human beings (the African man and woman) can produce two superior offspring (the European man and woman).

MYTH #3: *Mother Nature Is Clueless And Incompetent*

Mother Nature – the physical manifestation of GOD – gave every species – including humans -- the physical traits needed for survival. Europeans have straighter, longer hair that provides protection in a cold climate. Pale skin and light eyes indicates that whites have less melanin than more melanated people (of color), and also indicates a native environment where there was less exposure to intense, direct sunlight.

Mother Nature chose Africa as the birthplace of all humankind and chose the African man and woman to be the first people on earth. She equipped Africans with dark eyes, tightly spiraled hair, and the most melanin, which makes dark skin ideal for Africa's climate and intense heat and sunlight.

Light skin, hair, and eyes are more desirable in a cold climate with less intense sunlight since melanin blocks the absorption of sunlight. Bottom line, the differences in skin color for whites evolved due to natural selection, genetics, and environment, NOT racial or intellectual superiority.

MYTH #4: *One Beauty Standard (European) Fits All (Races)*

False. The physical differences between different ethnic groups are determined by genetics, the environment, and other biological factors. It is illogical (and insane) to judge all human beings by ONE beauty standard, just like it is insane (and illogical) to expect a Rottweiler to look like a Great Dane just because both are DOGS.

MYTH #5: *The European Beauty Standard Is A Universal Standard*

False. It is ILLOGICAL (and insane) for the white minority (10% of the people on the planet) to be the standard for what is normal or desirable for the other non-white 90%. In fact, today's (European) beauty standards are the exact opposite of the beauty standards that existed hundreds of years before white supremacy infected the planet:

Pre-Modern Asian Ideas On Race

The text below is reprinted from the article, *"Universal preference of whiteness over blackness?"* by colorq.org. (www.colorq.org/articles/article. aspx?d=1999&x=blackwhite).

"Standards of beauty in South and Southeast Asia: Marco Polo reports on the Dravidians of South India: "It is a fact that in this country when a child is born they anoint him once a week with oil of sesame, and this makes him grow much darker than when he was born."

"In the Chinese record Nan tsi Chou, a Chinese traveler to Southeast Asia wrote of the people: "...they consider black the most beautiful."

"Prior to European colonization, the ancient Visayans of the Philippines considered the very opposite of high noses and oval faces handsome. Visayans, as well as some other Austronesian peoples in Malaysia and Indonesia, compressed their babies' skulls to achieve broad faces and flat noses."

Old Chinese Views On Caucasians

The text below is reprinted from the article, *"Universal preference of whiteness over blackness?"* -- courtesy of www.colorq.org.

By traditional Chinese opera conventions, a black face is considered nobler. Actors wear masks that denote the character's qualities. A predominantly black face indicates courage, righteousness, and incorruptibility. A predominantly white face indicates craftiness, deceit, and knavery.

Ming Dynasty China records even state that Caucasians, especially blondes, are physically unattractive: "Huihui are shaggy with big noses, and Qipchags have light hair and blue eyes. Their appearance is vile and peculiar, so there are those (Chinese) who do not wish to marry them."

This distaste for blondes is a stark contrast to the worship of European standards of beauty so prevalent among modern Asians today.

The Character And Beauty Of Ethiopians Admired By Ancient Europeans

The text below is reprinted from the article, *"Universal preference of whiteness over blackness?"* -- courtesy of www.colorq.org.

"The Ethiopians," wrote Herodotos, "are said to be the tallest and best-looking people in the world." (In ancient Roman/Greek writings, the term "Ethiopian" is loosely used to refer to all black Africans).

Greek writer Diodoros wrote of the Ethiopians: "Their piety has been published abroad among all men, and it is generally held that the sacrifices practiced among the Ethiopians are those which are the most pleasing to heaven."

If Europeans were living back in ancient times, they might be searching for cosmetic remedies to darken their skin and kink up their hair – like the millions of whites today who flock to beaches and tanning salons to darken their skin; to plastic surgeons to thicken their lips, and enlarge breasts and buttocks; and to hair salons to perm, wave, kink, and curl their hair.

MYTH #6: *Africans Worshipped The First Europeans As "Gods"*

False. Contrary to the racist delusions of Hollywood moviemakers, Africans did not think the first Europeans were gods (or goddesses). Some Africans believed Europeans were white because they had been skinned alive.

Others, like **Olaudah Equiano**, was terrified by the appearance of the white men who kidnapped him from his African village and brought him to the New World on a slaveship in 1756.

After ten years of enslavement, Olaudah purchased his freedom and wrote his autobiography, describing the horrors of slavery, the cruelty of slaveowners, and how he fainted with fright the first time he saw the *"... white men with horrible looks, red faces, and long hair..."*

In pre-colonial Africa, a skin-color inferiority complex was nonexistent. Africans took pride in their skin, hair, and features because it was desirable (normal) to look like their fathers, mothers, aunts, uncles, and grandparents.

Africans never knew they were "inferior" **until the Europeans colonized (conquered) Africa,** and used physical differences to justify enslaving, robbing, raping, and murdering them. Only after four centuries of being FORCE-FED these artificially created (false) European beauty standards, Africans, and their descendants, learned to hate what they saw in the mirror.

MYTH #7: *It Is Normal For One Race To Think A Different Race Is More Attractive (Superior)*

False. It is ABNORMAL to view another race as more attractive, just like it is ABNORMAL to look into a mirror and see ugliness. A black child will not automatically think pale skin is superior to his skin, any more than a white child thinks his pale skin is inferior. Every child – regardless of race -- has a healthy amount of self-esteem until he or she is *taught* to feel inferior.

What Happened To "Black Is Beautiful?"

The slogan, "Black is beautiful," which became popular in the 1970s, was little more than a good idea turned bad fad. By the time non-black merchandisers, the blax-ploitation filmmakers, and the media made a fortune from *Superfly* hats, high-heeled shoes, idiotic films, and afro combs, "black and proud" became synonymous with "black and foolish."

We did not understand why such a wonderful slogan had been doomed from the start. We did not understand that we had to scrape off the rusted paint of self-hatred and inferiority before we applied a new paint job. We did not understand that in order to REDO, we first had to *UNDO.*

The telltale sign of past or present European colonization of a non-white nation: the people become self-hating.

If European (white supremacy) beauty standards had not been literally rammed down the throats of millions of Asians, it is doubtful a single Asian woman would correct a NONEXISTENT flaw by undergoing eye surgery to make her slanted eyes rounder, and more "Western" (European).

If European beauty standards had not been literally rammed down the throats of Africans and Indians (and their descendants), it is doubtful a single non-white man or woman would even think of using bleaching creams or swallowing poisonous pills, risking skin cancer, leukemia, thyroid disorders, and leprosy to lighten (destroy) the most age-resistant skin on earth.

MYTH #8: Black women are more obese than non-black women

False. Hispanic women have a higher obesity rate than black or white females:

"When percent body fat was used, the obesity rate was highest in Hispanic women (69.1%) and the rates were similar in white (58.7%) and black women (60.4%)."
-- http://journals.lww.com/greenjournal/Fulltext/2010/05000/Accuracy_of_Current_Body_Mass_Index_Obesity.17.aspx
(The American College of Obstretricians And Gynecologists)

***

A 2011 REUTERS HEALTH STUDY BY THE PENNINGTON BIOMEDICAL RESEARCH CENTER

"..a BMI (Body Mass Indexes) of 30 or higher is linked to more cases of high cholesterol, diabetes and high blood pressure. But Katzmarzyk found that the cut-off does not seem to hold true for black women. While there was no racial difference for men, Katzmarzyk showed that, for black women, the risk didn't increase until they reached a BMI of 33.

For example, for a 5'5" tall woman, the statistical risk for disease would increase at 180 pounds if she was white but at 198 pounds if she was black. A black woman can be healthy with a bigger waistline as well, according to the study. Dr. Katamarzyk thought a possible reason for the contrast might be the difference in the way body fat is distributed in women among the races." (2011)

http://caloriecount.about.com/study-shows-black-women-can-healthy-b493869

A 1991 survey commissioned by the American Association of University Women, discovered that little girls lose their self-esteem by adolescence. The study also found that black girls were still self-confident in high school compared to white and Hispanic girls.

Researchers concluded that black parents may be teaching their children that there is nothing wrong with them, only with the way the world treated them.

"This should encourage white people to look with admiration at the black community," said Dr. Linda Kerber, a history professor at the University of Iowa.

AFTER the study that claimed black girls had higher self-esteem than white girls, the mainstream media launched a FULL-ON ASSAULT against the black female image that continues to this day.

A coincidence OR by design?

MYTH #9: Black Females Have Lower Self-Esteem Than Non-Black Females

False: Despite the massive inferiority programming of black females from cradle to grave, black women generally have a more positive body image than Caucasian females, according to a Washington University study.

In addition, black women with **a strong sense of black identity** actually rated themselves more attractive than pictures of supposedly beautiful white fashion models, and 40% of black women rated their figures to be attractive or very attractive.

In the March 2011 issue of Allure magazine, 2,000 women were polled about their beauty preferences and discovered that black women were happier with their bodies, and were twice as likely to report NOT wanting to change their body in any way when compared to white women.

Other research indicates that black women are more flexible in their concepts of beauty than their white counterparts, who express rigid ideals and greater dissatisfaction with their own body-shapes. Another survey found black girls were more self-confident in high school than either white or Hispanic girls, and that white girls lost their self-confidence at an earlier age than Hispanic girls.

Black girls with **a strong sense of black identity** do not define themselves by (false) white beauty standards. Nor are they totally dependent on looks for self-esteem, but rely on other factors like personality, style, and intelligence. A black girl who is black-identified (instead of white-identified) knows there is nothing inherently wrong with being black; and is less likely to mutilate or surgically alter her body.

Which explains why so many black females view the eating disorders (like bulimia and anorexia) that afflict the white female population with puzzlement and contempt. Black females, in general, do not long for rail thin arms and legs or tiny butts. Their opinion of a sexy body is far more generous and forgiving since perfection is never a requirement.

Black females also have less of a tendency to obsess over minor flaws in their appearance. However, if a black female is white-identified, she may mimic the self-hating behavior of her white peers, although seldom to the same extreme degree.

How can black females have HIGHER SELF-ESTEEM than white females in a white supremacy system where the black female occupies the bottom rung of the beauty totem pole?

The same resilience that allowed black females to survive **400 YEARS OF SLAVERY, BRUTALITY, AND MASS RAPE** may provide some protective armor against the psychological onslaught of a racist mainstream media that is determined to INFERIORIZE them.

MYTH #10: White People Benefit From The White Supremacy Beauty Standard

False. The BEAUTY CON GAME has boomeranged on the very ones it was supposed to benefit by breeding an unhealthy obsession with the exterior rather than the more important interior. This obsession is the primary reason there is so much unhappiness within the white collective over minor (and nonexistent) flaws in their own appearances.

Ironically, even though whites are supposed to be the most attractive people on the planet (in a system of white supremacy), they are also the most dissatisfied with their own appearance -- and the MOST INSECURE.

This predominantly white obsession with appearance (perfection) can be seen in the endless snake-oil advertisements for the billion-dollar beauty industry. For the promise of whiter (perfect) teeth, perfect noses, chins, thighs, abs, stomachs, lips, hair, skin, bigger breasts, wrinkle-free skin, potions, lotions, and the promise of staying young forever, millions of Americans swallow billions of pills and voluntarily go under the knife.

This obsession with perfection is also apparent in the epidemic of eating disorders that are most common among the white female population, who ironically, are also held up as the standard of feminine beauty for non-white females.

Is the obsession to be "perfect" (superior) undermining the white female's self-esteem rather than building it up?

White Beauty Standards Are Contemptuous Of ALL Women

Would a culture that truly values its females create a beauty standard that demoralizes and penalizes them? The answer is clear: *it does not value them; but in fact, secretly despises, even hates them.*

This contempt is obvious, given the widespread slaughter of white females **for entertainment and for profit in television, movies, and in real life.**

The white supremacy "beauty standards" actually demonstrate MORE contempt for white females than admiration. A culture that promotes a media-manufactured body ideal -- tall, long-legged, blonde, and bone-thin with zero-body-fat (a boy's body) -- that drives white girls and women to literally starve themselves to death is ANTI-WOMAN -- not woman-loving OR woman-respecting.

This is NOT about empathizing with whites, who are victims by their OWN HAND. This is NOT about empathizing with white females who use the same racist standards to elevate themselves above non-white females.

This is about exposing the BLATANT CONTRADICTIONS of a white beauty standard that even the WHITE CREATORS cannot measure up to.

Is the epidemic of self-loathing the karmic price the white collective is paying for perpetuating mass self-loathing among non-whites?

America is one of the wealthiest nations in the world YET Americans are plagued by more self-doubt, self-hatred, self-abuse, over-materialism, dysfunctional relationships, broken families, cruelty, jealousy, envy, bullying, vanity, narcissism, eating disorders, self-mutilation, drug and alcohol addiction, mental illness, depression, suicide, sexual deviancy, rape, incest, and homicide – than anywhere else – including the (so-called) Third World.

If the most privileged people on the planet are also the most miserable, they are missing the two most valuable lessons of their lives:

1. There is NO substitution for genuine self-respect and self-esteem. If we are mistreating others, we will have neither.
2. If we escape punishment for our ill deeds and crimes, ultimately, we will find a way to punish ourselves.

"Hi everyone, I've never posted anything, but I had to get this off my chest...

Let me start by saying that I'm 20, and I'm a dark -skinned sista. Up until my current relationship, nobody I have dated ever made any reference to my skin tone (I am not ashamed of my color, I just don't think it should be an issue in whether or not a person wants to talk to me).

On Sunday, while I was chilling in my boyfriend's room, his homeboy comes in and they start talking about girls. His boy looks at me and tells me that I'm pretty for a dark-skinned girl. My boyfriend jumps in and starts talking about how light-skinned women are so beautiful, how dark women are ugly, and how he should have gone to Southern (which is known for its light-skinned girls; we both go to Grambling).

He's been doing this a lot lately. It's confusing, as this is something he never did when we first started going out together. I've read about things like this happening to other people, but nothing compares to being face-to-face with it.

What I want to know is, has something like this ever happened to anybody else, and if so, what did you do? Give me some advice on what I should do; all help is welcome. Please, no light- or dark-skinned people bashing, as this is not the purpose of this post.

-- posted on a black website in 2009

CHAPTER SEVEN

HOW THE LANGUAGE OF WHITE SUPREMACY PENALIZES BLACK FEMALES

The white supremacy culture defines "beauty" by what is normal and the most desirable for white people: pale skin, hair, and eyes. This combination is considered the most beautiful -- especially for white females.

This color bias can be found in commonly known phrases such as, *"she was the fairest (lightest) in all the land"* and *"the fairer sex."* The word *"fair" then* becomes synonomous with *"white, beautiful, and feminine"* meaning the white female is the most feminine and the most beautiful compared to non-white females.

The lightest (fairest) female who is blond, blue-eyed, and pale-skinned occupies the top rung of the beauty pedestal because she helps to maintain the illusion of white superiority. She is always assumed to be beautiful, regardless of how attractive or unattractive; or extraordinary or ordinary that particular pale-skinned, blue-eyed blonde may be.

The irony (and gross contradiction) of this FALSE beauty standard is the most beautiful blondes in Hollywood history -- Jean Harlow, Jayne Mansfield, Marilyn Monroe, Loni Anderson, and Pamela Sue Anderson – **were born brunettes.** The reverse is true for male attractiveness, where the most masculine, and most sexually desirable male in a white supremacy society is often described as *"...tall, dark, and handsome."*

This definition of "male beauty" may give the dark-skinned black male an advantage in the proverbial bedroom BUT it puts him at a distinct disadvantage in the social and corporate arena. It also serves to connect the word *"dark"* with the word *"masculine,"* which illustrates how the language of white supremacy PENALIZES the dark-skinned black female.

The Triple Demons Of Racism, Sexism, and Colorism

The black female in a white supremacy system is victimized by the triple demons of RACISM, SEXISM, and COLORISM, and faces more discrimination than any other person on the planet.

The black female is confronted on a daily basis by a hostile white and black world that systematically degrades AND denies her natural beauty. Starting as young as four or five, little black girls are taught that dark skin is unattractive and black hair is "bad hair," and must be straightened or hidden beneath a wig or a weave to look more "presentable" (less black).

Even The "Justice" System Penalizes Dark-Skinned Females

"A recent study of women prisoners in North Carolina found that lighter-skinned Black inmates served less time than darker-skinned Black ones.

"The Impact of Light Skin on Prison Time for Black Female Offenders," by Jill Viglione, Lance Hannon, and Robert DeFina of Villanova University, used a sample of 12, 158 women who were imprisoned between 1995 and 2009.

Those who were perceived to be light skinned received sentences that were, on average, 12% shorter than their darker counterparts. The amount of actual time served was approximately 11% less."

(SOURCE: Lighter Skin Equals Shorter Sentences For Black Female Prisonershttp://racismdaily.com/2011/06/22/study-lighter-skin-equals-shorter-sentences-for-black-female-prisoners/

These destructive messages follows black females into their adult years. The black female seldom sees her own unique, NATURAL beauty positively reflected on the TV screen, magazine ads, music videos, or as the romantic female lead in a motion picture because *dark, feminine, and beautiful contradicts the lie of white (female) supremacy.*

Because of her consistently cruel treatment at the hands of whites AND blacks, the black female has a sometimes well-deserved reputation for having a *"bad attitude."*

This "bad attitude" is largely a reaction AND a defense mechanism against a black-hating, female-hating, and black-female-hating world that is often perceived (correctly) by the black female as hostile and threatening to her self-esteem, physical safety, and psychological survival.

Do not misinterpret anything said here as pity for the black woman. This is not an attempt to make excuses for bad behavior, or an attempt to speak for black women. *The black female is not to be pitied; she is to be admired.*

Despite her cruel treatment over the last 500 years, the black female's style, language, innovation, creativity, courage, dancing and musical talents, intellectual brilliance, dignity, AND physical features *are imitated AND duplicated all over the world by NON-BLACK FEMALES.*

An (Unconscious) Black Celebration Of Self-Hatred

"It's like when you have coffee and it's too Black, it's too strong. So you have to add milk to it. You add enough milk you completely weaken it. If you add too much milk you won't even know you had coffee anymore." – Malcolm X

In the black community the light-skinned female OR black female with a white parent is uplifted as the ultimate sex symbol (because she looks more white) while the dark-skinned female is seen as sexual chattel, and the butt of ignorant, self-hating "black" humor.

In Toni Morrison's novel, *The Bluest Eye*, Pecola Breedlove, a little black girl, believed that if she were white, the world would be hers. In Alice Walker's novel, *The Color Purple*, Celie was told (by another black person) that she would never be anything because she is *"poor, black, ugly, and a woman."*

When we disrespect black females because they are NOT WHITE ENOUGH, we are worshipping (and submitting to) white supremacy AND *advertising our own self-hatred and anti-blackness.*

Instead of celebrating the PURITY and RICHNESS of our melanin that the black female's beautiful dark skin represents, we are celebrating -- in our IGNORANCE -- the infusion of white blood into our genetic pool even when it came about as a result of *400 years of rape.* We are not only celebrating slave traditions, *we are celebrating SLAVE-OWNER TRADITIONS.*

"Ethnic" + "Exotic" = NON-WHITE

"If I say, exotic beauty, who is the first person you picture? I'll be honest and say it's the Brazilian Victoria's Secret model, Adriana Lima. Dark flowing hair, full lips, tanned skin, and cool bluish-green eyes. A look that is exotic, otherworldly." -- Goal Auzeen Saedi in Millennial Media (SOURCE: http://www.psychologytoday.com/blog/ millenial-media/201104/what-is-exotic-beauty-part-i)

In a white supremacy society, a sexually attractive non-white female is often described as **"ethnic" and/or "exotic-looking."** An example, would be a non-white female with a white parent and an Asian parent who is attractive by white standards. However, if we examine the Webster dictionary's definition of **"exotic"** it is clear this label is FAR from a compliment:

Exotic: strikingly unusual, strange in effect or appearance, or other-worldly; somebody or something unusual and striking; an exotic species; a person or a thing that is foreign or unusual.

The term **"ethnic"** usually refers to brown and black females, while **"exotic"** usually refers to non-white females who either have a white parent, or are classified as white with a "taint" of non-white heritage.

White people DO NOT refer to themselves OR other white people as **"ethnic"** or **"exotic,"** even though Webster's defines **"ethnic"** as *"a large group of people classed according to common racial, national, religious, or cultural origins."*

In addition, since whites represent ONLY eight percent of the world's population, they would more easily fall into the category of "exotic, un-usual, or otherworldly" than the other NON-WHITE 92% majority.

What is the main reason non-white females are labeled "ethnic" or "exotic?" ***To prevent the sexually attractive non-white fe-male from DIRECTLY COMPETING with the white female.***

To illustrate this point, the American music awards industry created separate categories for "black music" and "white music" -- such as R&B, Rock, and Pop, even though the FOUNDATION of ALL modern American music is BLACK MUSIC.

Creating separate categories of music protects white musical artists from DIRECTLY COMPETING with black artists, and from possibly losing to their often superior (black) competition.

Does this mean all white musical artists are inferior to all black artists? Not necessarily, but creating separate categories for beauty and music does ***reveal a deep-seated fear of honest competition and comparison.***

"I am black woman, and I'm tired of being told we have 'bad attitudes.' Who wouldn't have a bad attitude if they were always being put down and told they were ugly and undesirable?

What's amazing is so many of us still have any sense of humor at all after dealing with all this negative nonsense about who we are and what we look like.

The second most amazing thing is black women still rate higher than white, Asian, and Hispanic women when it comes to high self-esteem and feeling good about ourselves and our bodies -- no matter how much whites put us down.

No one else could handle this kind of pressure without going crazy. That says a lot about who we are and why we might be such a threat that they have to keep a foot on our necks. Viva la black woman!"

Pamela, 44, blogger

CHAPTER EIGHT

STOLEN BLACK BEAUTY

According to the 2009 American Society of Plastic Surgeons report, females accounted for 91 PERCENT of all cosmetic procedures. The most popular include breast augmentation, lip augmentation, facelifts, skin laser treatments, and butt implants.

European beauty standards have always associated full lips with beauty, youth, and sexuality -- which explains why the western medical/beauty industry is FRANTIC to create methods to duplicate them.

For example, around 1900, surgeons injected paraffin (wax) into the lips of white females *without success*. Liquid silicone was used in the 1960s to enhance lips until the fears about silicone stopped the practice. Currently, cosmetic surgeons are working on a procedure that allows them to use segments of neck muscle as lip grafts to "plump" them up.

Obviously, cost is no deterrent when it comes to MIMICKING THE BEAUTY OF BLACK FEMALES since *a single collagen lip treatment can cost up to $400 per injection*, and "lip enhancement" procedures can range anywhere from $500 to $5,000.

It is UNDENIABLE that the black female's round buttocks, full breasts, voluptuous lips, and age-resistant (melanated) skin are among the most prized and coveted physical features among the white female collective.

The proof: the mass-production and mass-implementation of *the black female's uniquely beautiful racial characteristics* gross hundreds of millions of dollars for plastic surgeons every year.

In light of the above FACTS, how can the black female still be the MOST DEGRADED FEMALE on the planet?

One logical answer:

Black Females Must Be Inferior In A White Supremacy System

Openly acknowledging the beauty of the dark-skinned black female breaks the fundamental rule of the White Supremacy Beauty Con Game:

A non-white female cannot be equal OR superior to the white female.

This explains why the black female's most coveted features -- full lips, breasts, and buttocks -- had to be DISCONNECTED from the black female and RECONNECTED to a white (or a near white) female using the awesome power (propaganda) of the white media.

However, the *illusion* of the superior white female flies in the face of the REALITY of butt implants, breast implants, face-lifts, liposuction, chin implants, curly perms, collagen lip injections, Botox, nose jobs, hair weaves, colorful skin and eye makeup, cancer-causing suntans, and tanning salons to add COLOR to pale skin.

This blatant IMITATION and DUPLICATION of the "inferior" black female's features explains why the white media feverishly promotes the "round buttocks" of (a white-looking) Jennifer Lopez and the "big lips" of actress Angelina Jolie: *to CLAIM and RE-NAME "black beauty" in the name of "whiteness."*

It also explains WHY the uniquely beautiful features of the black female have been targeted for ridicule by the white media, clearly ignoring the hundreds of thousands of white females who pay thousands of dollars, risking their health, and in some cases their lives, to undergo risky plastic surgery and skin-tanning -- *to look LESS white.*

Which brings to mind a CRITICAL (and revealing) question:

If the black female is the least attractive female in a white supremacy society, why would her unique physical characteristics be the most sought-after cosmetic and surgical procedures by the MOST attractive (white) female?

In a system of white supremacy, IMITATION is NOT a form of flattery BUT it does expose the LIE and reveal the TRUTH.

"Alas I melt as wax at the sight of her beauty. She is black, it is true, but what matters? Coals are black; but when they are alight they glow like rose cups."

-- Asclepiades, 270 B.C. (Greece)

"Regarding the 'Kim Kardashian effect,' the first thing that comes to my lips is, "You've got to be kidding me." But of course I know this is all too real.

The same features that are ridiculed on a black woman all of a sudden become attractive on a white woman? Do you know how many times I've heard white people comment on how over-sized-black women's butts are, but a white woman has the same thing and she's voluptuous!

The reason all this just came to mind, I was logging into my yahoo account and one of the stories was the hottest women of all time. I don't even have to look to know that it's exclusively white with a light-skinned girl or two that fits their profile of beauty thrown in as a token.

I have to get back to work.

Robert, 43, systems technician

Wisconsin Congressman Jim Sensenbrenner, referring to First Lady Michelle Obama's efforts to combat childhood obesity, said, "...she lectures us on eating right..." then added, "And look at her big butt." (December, 2011)

***

If a white female has a big butt, it's sexy, but when a black woman has a curvaceous figure like Mrs. Obama, she's ridiculed by white people just for having a shape or showing off her arms. They refuse to respect black women even when she's the First Lady of the United States!

White people know black women are the standard for lips, curves, and butts, but they're too racist to admit it or give us credit. Look at all these white homosexual Congressmen and coaches getting busted "out of the closet" and all these bitchy comments white males are making about black females, it almost sounds like jealousy, like some kind of male bitchery."

-- Carla, 52

The 'Hottentot Venus' (1810)

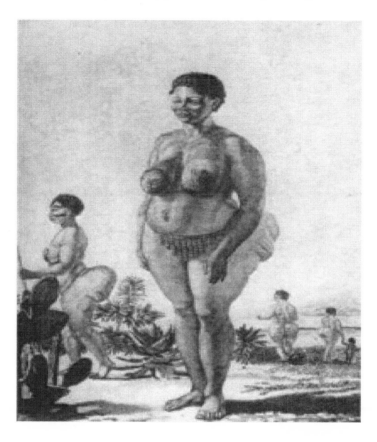

In 1810, Saartjie Baartman, known as the Hottentot Venus, was lured from her South African village with promises of becoming wealthy and famous. Baartman was sold to a French animal trainer, Regu, who exhibited her (like a circus act).

She was exploited, ridiculed due to her unique anatomy (by white standards), and forced to entertain white spectators by shaking her buttocks. Once the "novelty" wore off, she allegedly began to drink heavily and support herself with prostitution.

She died in 1815, penniless and heartbroken. Even death offered no relief from humiliation and exploitation. Her brain and genitals were put on display in Paris until 1974.

South African president, Nelson Mandela, formally requested that France return her remains. She was buried in her homeland on May 6, 2002 on a hill in the town on Hankey more than 200 years after she was born.

The 'Hottentot Venus' (1810)

Several figures bend straining for a better look, while a male figure at the far right of the image even holds his seeing-eye glass up to better behold the woman's body. The European observers remark on the woman's body: *"Oh! God Damn what roast beef!"* and *"Ah! how comical is nature."*

***

Several prints dating from the early nineteenth century illustrate the sensation generated by the spectacle of "The Hottentot Venus." A French print entitled "La Belle Hottentot," for example, depicts the Khosian woman standing with her buttocks exposed on a box-like pedestal.

White Fashions Inspired by the 'Hottentot Venus'

Polanaise costume, 1883   'The Parisian' by Pierre-Auguste Renoir (1874)

Decades after her death, the Hottentot Venus inspired white females from America to Europe to adopt fashions that gave them the appearance of having protruding buttocks (like the "inferior" black female's). This "imitation" is obvious once a comparison is made between the artificially created costumes and the natural figure of the Saartjie Bartman (the Hottentot Venus).

Straight Talk About Nappy Hair

CHAPTER NINE

STRAIGHT TALK
ABOUT NAPPY HAIR

"Don't remove the kinks from your HAIR. Remove them from your BRAIN." -- *The Honorable Marcus Mosiah Garvey (1887-1940)*

Baby, Let Your Hair Hang Down

Audrey was sitting across a candlelit table from Ernest, a man she met the week before on the commuter train to work. She had dressed carefully for their first date. Not too plain-jane but not too sexy. She didn't want him to think she was willing to trade her body for a glass of wine and a plate of blackened tilapia.

The conversation had been decent but nothing special. Audrey had been hoping for some kind of spark then warned herself to relax and just enjoy the man's company. That was the problem with single women like herself; they expected an instant connection with a man they just met. For all she knew, Ernest was having the same doubts about her.

"This fish is delicious," Audrey said, letting him know she appreciated the meal he was paying for.

"Not as delicious as you," Ernest said, bold brown eyes staring over his raised cocktail glass.

"You know what they say. Appearances can be deceiving," Audrey teased, refusing to take his comment seriously. She was a little flattered by his constant staring, but also a little unnerved. Finally, she asked, "Is something wrong?"

"Wrong?"

"You keep staring."

"Just wondering..." His voice trailed off, a wistful look on his face.

"About what?" Audrey mentally crossed her fingers. *Please don't let this man say something stupid.*

"I was wondering what you'd look like if you let your hair down."

"Let my what down?" She sat back, frowning.

"It's sexy," Ernest continued. "When a woman lets her hair down." He tilted his head back and rolled his shoulders to demonstrate.

"Uh-huh," Audrey said, a self-conscious hand straying to the French roll she'd plastered with hair goo to keep the short, stray hairs lying flat.

"If I was your man, would you let your hair down for me?"

"But, see, you're not my man, so I don't have to answer that," Audrey said firmly.

"I might be one day."

Why was this man going there on their first date? And why was the fool talking about letting her hair down when it barely reached her shoulders?

Unfortunately, Audrey knew exactly what Ernest meant. If she had seen that tired scene once, she had seen it a hundred times:

The prim and proper, plain-Jane white female, hair in a tight bun, glasses, white blouse buttoned up to her chin, who hadn't had sex since the Great Depression. The handsome male hero walks in the door. Bam! Instant attraction! The top buttons of her blouse pop loose. She reaches up and pulls out that one strategically placed hairpin, shakes her head, and her long hair tumbles around her face, transforming her from a frigid librarian into a raging sex kitten!

When Audrey was younger, she wanted long hair like that, but now, just a few days short of her 40th birthday, she was no longer impressed with Hollywood's idea of sexy. She thought it fake, silly, and too contrived. In fact, spending so much time and money fretting, fixing, and worrying about her hair was wearing on her last nerve.

She was sick of waiting for hours at the beauty salon, sick of hair relaxers, hair straighteners, and hair rollers. She was sick of trying to stretch, pull, and shape her short hair into a decent style every morning. Audrey had decided that this would be the year to throw away the relaxers and curling irons, and start wearing her hair natural. And now this clown wanted to turn her into a piss-poor imitation of a white female?

Ten years ago, Ernest's careless comment would have made her feel inadequate – or it might have driven her to the nearest hair weave salon to accommodate his inappropriate, and frankly, rude expectations. Ernest had no idea how much he had turned her off, or that this would be their last date, because he was still smiling and waiting for her response.

"Ernie," Audrey cooed, giving him a seductive smile. "I'll let my hair down on one condition."

"What?" Ernest leaned forward, an eager look on his face.

"You let your hair grow long and silky, so I can run my fingers through it." Then Audrey's eyes traveled slowly and deliberately up to the balding spot on top of his thinning, close-cropped, nappy fade.

THE END

CHAPTER TEN

THE "JOY" OF
NAPPY HUMOR

Don Imus and his "crew" take aim at the hair and sexual morality of eight black teenaged girls on the Rutgers basketball team (April 4, 2007).

IMUS (host): So, I watched the basketball game last night between --
a little bit of Rutgers and Tennessee, the women's final.
ROSENBERG (former Imus sports announcer): Yeah, Tennessee won
last night -- seventh championship for Pat Summitt, I-Man. They beat
Rutgers by 13 points.
IMUS: That's some rough girls from Rutgers. Man, they got tattoos --
McGUIRK (producer): Some hard-core hos.
IMUS: That's some nappy-headed hos there. I'm gonna tell you that
now, man, that's some -- woo. And the girls from Tennessee, they all
look cute...
McGUIRK: A Spike Lee thing.
IMUS: Yeah.
McGUIRK: The Jigaboos vs. the Wannabes -- that movie he had.
IMUS: Yeah, it was a tough --
McCORD (newsman): Do The Right Thing.
McGUIRK: Yeah, yeah, yeah.
IMUS: I don't know if I'd have wanted to beat Rutgers or not, but they
did, right?
ROSENBERG: It was a tough watch. The more I look at Rutgers, they
look exactly like the Toronto Raptors.
RUFFINO (engineer): Only tougher.
McGUIRK: The [Memphis] Grizzlies would be more appropriate.

Nappy hair has been a frequent target of white ridicule. There is a tremendous amount of pressure for black women to imitate a beauty standard that was designed for white women. This makes hair a sensitive topic for many black females. Even though black males are not pressured to have long hair, straight hair, "good hair," or any hair at all, they are just as obsessive (and conflicted) about "black hair." One only has to turn the clock back 40 years to recall the "conk" hairstyles that were once popular among black males.

Let's Take A Short Walk Down Memory Lane...

Malcolm X On The "Conk" Hairstyle

"This was the first really big step toward self-degradation: when I endured all of that pain, literally burning my flesh, to have it look like a white man's hair.

I had joined that multitude of Negro men and women in America who are brainwashed into believing that the black people are 'inferior' and the white people 'superior' - that they will even violate and mutilate their God-created bodies to try to look 'pretty' by white standards.

Look around today, in every small town and big city, from two-bit catfish and soda-pop joints into the 'integrated' lobby of the Waldorf-Astoria, and you'll see conks on black men, and black women wearing these green and pink and purple and red and platinum blonde wigs.

They're all more ridiculous than a slapstick comedy. It makes you wonder if the Negro has completely lost his sense of identity, lost touch with himself."

The "Conk" Hairstyle

"The "conk" was a popular hairstyle for black men from the 1920s to the 1960s. The naturally "kinky" hair would be chemically straightened using lye, and styled into pompadours that resembled white hairstyles.

Some men chose to simply slick their straightened hair back to lie flat on their heads (like white males). At home, a "do-rag" (head wrap or scarf) had to be worn to prevent sweat and other situations to prevent the "conked" hair from reverting back to its natural (nappy) state. Relaxers had to be constantly reapplied as new hair grew in.

If the conk was a form of self-degradation for the black male, are hair straighteners, perms, and hair weaves inflicting the same kind of self-esteem damage on the unsuspecting black female?

A Classic Case Of The Pot Calling The Kettle "Nappy"

Despite the black male's own history of hair obsession, he is quick to belittle black women for all the time and money they spend on their hair, forgetting that HE is the one who rewards black females who come the closest to the white beauty standard.

Some black males' hypocritical and contradictory "pride" in their own blackness may not be extended to black women who refuse to straighten their hair (imitate white beauty), and proudly and defiantly wear their natural hair short, braided, locked or dreadlocked.

Black females who wear their naturally nappy hair often run the risk of being labeled as less feminine and less attractive by black males than their long, and permed-hair female peers.

When black women try to live up (or down) to the unreasonable standards FORCED upon them by white society and by black males (who often openly admire "white features"), they are ridiculed for wearing hair weaves, wigs, and "horse hair."

Some black male comedians -- who wear their OWN hair in locks as a sign of so-called "racial pride" -- often use black women's hair as the butt of their "unbeweavable" and "nappy hair" humor.

"Now they aren't 'hos,' but there were some nappy-headed women on that team. Those are some of the ugliest women I've ever seen in my whole life." -- black comic D.L. Hughley on Jay Leno's "Tonight Show" (May 7, 2007), "joking" about the black girls on the Rutgers University Basketball team.

Three FACTS (some) black males conveniently ignore: (1) the black female's hair is the SAME HAIR THAT GROWS OUT OF THEIR OWN SCALPS, (2) their GENES are *50 percent responsible for the hair of the black female*, and (3) their ridicule of (and contempt for) the black female's hair is **an ANNOUNCEMENT of their contempt for themselves, their genetics, and the hair on their own heads.**

Men Set the Beauty Standards For Every Culture

In male-dominated cultures (like America) men, NOT women, set the standards for feminine beauty. Once this "beauty standard" is established, the women fall in line by conforming (or trying to conform) to these standards.

The most powerful males in a male-dominated society use the most desirable females to enhance their status in the eyes of other males. The women strike a similar bargain, trading their youth (fertility), and beauty (high status) for financial security (marriage).

Do not confuse 'status" with validation. In a male-dominated society, women CANNOT validate men; *only men can validate other men*. The same is true for women in a male-dominated society. Women *do not validate* women; they COMPETE with other women. Only men can validate women.

Make no mistake. The black community is a male-dominated society. It does not matter that black females head up almost 70% of black households. That is an economic and political reality (tragedy), NOT a cultural choice.

Like all males in a male-dominated society (like America) most males, in general, reject female leadership. However, most women -- and black women are no exception -- actually welcome male leadership. In other words, most black women will follow black men, but most black men will not follow black women. The proof:

1. the preacher
2. the politician
3. the pimp

Whether it is the church, the meeting hall, or the street corner, black men usually lead; black women usually follow. With a few exceptions, black women are the foot soldiers and seldom the generals in most black organizations.

When it comes to female beauty standards, black males -- like all males in a male-dominated society -- decide what is desirable and what is not. In nearly every culture in the world, the women always look to the men of their culture to **validate** their self-worth and their value as women. Why is this so important to understand?

Because males collectively have the power to psychologically devastate females collectively if they do not validate their worth AS females.

For example, the white male supremacist elevates the thin, blonde, blue-eyed, and pale-skinned female because she has the highest genetic value in a society that prizes "whiteness" and "lightness."

White females are programmed from childhood to accept this narrowly defined beauty standard, and will judge their own beauty (value) as females by this standard.

To attract men (a desirable mate), millions of white females imitate (or try to imitate) the beauty standard set by white males so they can be *validated* (and socially, financially, and romantically rewarded) by white males. We know this is true from the astronomical number of white females (of all ages and incomes) who dye their hair blond and starve themselves to be thin.

The black(?) beauty standard for black females -- light skin, long hair, and European features -- is based on the same white supremacy standards. Black females learn the painful lesson at an early age that the most powerful and influential black males – as well as many average and ordinary black males -- "reward" black females who are closer in appearance to the white standard of beauty. The proof:

The light-skinned, Asian, white wives and girlfriends of the most influential and successful (status-seeking) black men.

Black Male Invalidation Of Black Females

Detroit headline: A local DJ and club promoter cancels party that would let "light-skinned" black women into the club for free (2007)

In their attempt to gain status, some black males seek validation from the male with the highest status in a white supremacy society -- **the powerful white male.**

When the black male deliberately chooses the female with the highest status (the white or white-appearing female) -- he is **unconsciously reinforcing his own inferiority** as a non-white person.

Even if she does not articulate it, the black female knows **instinctively** that the black male's (foolish) choice of (white) status over honoring his female mirror image is **unjust**, and is the greatest possible betrayal that a man can commit against the women of his race.

This unspoken (but obvious) resentment accounts for a great deal of the black woman's anger toward black men. If the black female cannot depend on the black male to validate her worth as a female, who then can she turn to for protection?

If the black male refuses to validate (and value) the black woman (the black womb), how can he validate and value himself? Perhaps this explains his callous disregard for the black female and why black males slaughter each other without hesitation.

In 2007, when Beyonce appeared on the cover of Sports Illustrated's annual "Swimsuit Issue," angry white readers demanded subscription cancellations.

One reason given by a white male subscriber: *"My daughters grew up identifying with the models in the Swimsuit Issue, and wanting to be like them. How is my daughter supposed to see herself in Beyonce?"*

The white male -- collectively -- understands the potentially devastating effect on the white female psyche when a non-white female is elevated above the white female -- even for something as trivial as a magazine cover.

White males understand, collectively, that in order to validate themselves, they must validate (and uplift) the white female (the white womb).

Together, this reinforces the VALUE of white life. The black male is encouraged to do just the opposite -- uplift white females and degrade black females -- yet the black male does not understand why **black life -- including his -- is so cheap.**

If black males took a page out of the white male's book, flipped their tragic (and self-genocidal) black scripts, and collectively embraced their female mirror images in all shades of brown and black, wearing a crown of natural hair, the companies that profit from hair weaves, wigs, permed-hair, and skin-bleaching products **would go out of business.**

Black males would then reap the rich psychological and spiritual rewards of LOVING THEMSELVES by elevating and honoring the (black) womb that delivered them into the world.

Bottom line: black males must accept some of the blame for the time, attention, anxiety, and insanity displayed by (some) black women about their hair.

How The Beauty Con Game Penalizes Black Males

"When you teach a man to hate his lips, the lips that God gave him, the shape of the nose that God gave him, the texture of the hair that God gave him, the color of the skin that God gave him, you've committed the worst crime that a race of people can commit." – Malcolm X

The black male's secret shame (of looking and being too black) explains his collective disrespect toward black females, and it explains why so many successful, status-seeking black males deliberately choose non-black females.

It has less to do with non-black women being more desirable and more to do with what non-black women represent to the self-esteem-starved black male who measures his success by white (male) standards.

The black man's (unreasonable and self-genocidal) resentment toward the black female may be due in part to him subconciously BLAMING her for delivering him -- literally -- as a black male into a black-male-hating white world.

Where Have All The Shampoo Girls Gone?

Recently, a black male blogger from Chicago wanted to know...

"Where are all the white girls I see in those TV shampoo commercials? I have never seen a white female in person who had the kind of hair I see in those commercials."

The glorious manes seen on TV require hair additions, weaves, falls, wigs, sophisticated lighting techniques, film and photo retouching, and artificial substances and devices to add volume, curl, density, color, and sheen to hair.

These media-manufactured (false) television images are the primary reason so many females (of all races) are so dissatisfied with the hair growing out of their scalps, and why so many women (of all races) chemically treat, process, lenthen, straighten, thicken, curl, wave, kink, and color their hair, or use a battalion of artificial devices to enhance it.

Different Is Beautiful

Black hair is unique when compared to the hair of many other races. It is only through the lens of white supremacy/ black inferiority that this difference becomes a demoralizing focal point for many blacks.

Mother Nature – the physical manifestation of God – made us perfect in God's sight. Our hair serves a sacred purpose in its natural state, growing up toward the sun, like a spiritual antenna that connects us to our Creator.

The self-loving black male and female embraces the softness, texture, durability, and versatility of black hair. They know "hair" can't cook, clean, make love, comfort us, earn a living, save a life, nurse us back to health, fix a flat tire or a leaky faucet, or raise a healthy, happy child.

They know that hair – be it long, short, curly, wavy, kinky or straight -- is only a small part of what makes a man or woman desirable. The self-loving black male and black female know from experience that a long head of hair shrinks in importance if what lies beneath the scalp is wholly unappealing.

"A person obsessed with the exterior is already inferior -- in his or her own mind." -- Umoja

Tyra Banks Swears Off Fake Hair For Her Show (August 23rd, 2009)

Tyra Banks will be keeping it real on her talk show this fall -- it being her hair. The host announced Monday that she's swearing off extensions on the New season, starting Sept. 8. "No fake hair at all!" she tweeted. "Will be the hair coming out of my scalp! For all to see!" In a press statement, she said the show aims to help women "own and rock what they've got and be...

Months After Her Announcement...

Tyra Banks Announces Her Show Will End After Current Season (December 28, 2009)

Wrapping at the end of its fifth season in the spring of 2010, it will be lights out for the show that brought viewers memorable weave-exposing, cellulite-revealing and tear-jerking moments. Banks will focus on the launch of Bankable Studios, a N.Y.-based film production company currently reviewing possible projects.

CHAPTER 11

WHY BLACK FEMALE ENTERTAINERS MUST WEAR WEAVES THAT LOOK LIKE WEAVES

"If your hair is relaxed, white people are relaxed. If your hair is nappy, they're not happy." -- Comedian Paul Mooney

In the spring of 2010, black filmmaker, Tyler Perry, hosted an hour-long show on the TV Guide channel to promote his new movie, *Why Did I Get Married, Too?* When the first cast member, Jill Scott, a talented singer and actress, joined Perry on the stage, she looked like a beautiful black queen in her curve-hugging black dress, and perfectly groomed afro.

However, as one of her scenes in the movie played across the screen, it was hard not to wonder (with dismay) why Ms. Scott had to wear such an unflattering weave instead wearing her own beautifully natural hair?

Miss Scott is not alone. It is extremely rare to see a black female entertainer wearing her own unprocessed hair that hasn't been straightened or isn't hidden beneath an expensive wig or a unrealistic-looking weave.

This is NOT intended to ridicule black females OR their hairstyles. It's true that white females enhance their natural hair with chemicals, weaves, and extensions. The difference is white females are ENHANCING -- NOT DISGUISING -- the ethnic characteristics of their natural hair.

The opposite is true for today's black female entertainers, who wear weaves that do NOT match their natural hair texture, length, or color. Another difference between black females and white females who wear weaves is the vast majority of weaves REINFORCE white -- NOT black -- beauty standards.

Is "Weave-Wearing" By Choice Or By Demand?

We propose it is the latter – that black female entertainers MUST WEAR UNBELIEVABLE WEAVES THAT LOOK LIKE WEAVES -- if they want to "make it" in the entertainment industry. How do unbelievable weaves **PROMOTE** white supremacy? There are seven obvious benefits:

BENEFIT #1 -- No matter how sexy, talented or beautiful a black female entertainer is, her UNBELIEVABLE WEAVE subtracts major beauty points and GUARANTEES that the beautiful black female will ***never be seen as competition or as a threat*** to the throne of white female supremacy.

BENEFIT #2 -- UNBELIEVABLE WEAVES make it appear that black females are imitating and envying the (superior) white female. Imitation may be the sincerest form of flattery BUT NOT when it DEGRADES the imitators.

BENEFIT #3 -- UNBELIEVABLE WEAVE-WEARING black females are the best advertising white supremacy can buy, and help maintain the illusion of the superior white female by promoting white supremacy beauty standards.

BENEFIT #4 -- The rich and famous UNBELIEVABLE WEAVE-WEARING black female celebrity is the MOST VISIBLE "role model" for young (and not so young), impressionable black females, which is easily observed by the distressing number of black females who wear unflattering, easily detectable, and unnatural-looking hair weaves.

BENEFIT #5 -- Wearing UNBELIEVABLE WEAVES destroys the self-esteem of the unsuspecting black female who knows (subconsciously) that the enhanced image in her mirror is based on something that is NOT REAL. This confirms in her own SUBCONSCIOUS MIND that her own beauty is NONEXISTENT.

BENEFIT #6 -- UNBELIEVABLE WEAVES program black boys AND black men to see black females as "fakes," frauds, second-rate, and wanna-be white females who do NOT like, respect, or value themselves.

The MAIN one who benefits from UNBELIEVABLE WEAVES is the white female who NOW looks like genuine article to black males. This reinforces her superiority, and the inferiority of the black female, and has a disastrous effect on black male/black female relationships.

BENEFIT #7 -- Black females make up the largest share of the *multi-billion-dollar hair-care industry, largely due to the explosion of hair weaves.*

According to the 16th annual report on "The Buying Power of Black America" by Target Marketing, a black consumer research firm, blacks spent almost the same amount **($7.4 billion)** on hair-care and personal products that we spent on education **($7.5 billion)**.

The same (white-owned) hair care companies that shunned black consumers in the past are dominating the black haircare market -- to the delight of some misguided black females, who may get a psychological boost from using haircare products DESIGNED for the white female's hair because it makes them feel more acceptable (and more beautiful) by white standards.

The black female hair-care market is the beauty industry's biggest (and most disrespected) CASH COW. This may explain why there are NO nationally advertised products designed for the NATURAL HAIR OF BLACK FEMALES.

Why are so many black females with natural hair-styles being harassed by airport security? We're the last people to fit the "terrorist" profile. There has never been a black female terrorist in the history of the U.S. but there have been plenty of white terrorists. I don't see airport security harassing white people with long or bushy hair.

Again, it certainly looks like 'somebody' is doing their damndest to discourage black females from wearing our own natural hair by humiliating us in public!

I think the whites who control the media enjoy seeing black females wearing crazy looking blonde weaves because it shows – proves – that we are still confused, still imitating them, and still white-identified.

Also, when black females proudly wear our own hair, it might be a sign that we are waking up to the white lie that we're inferior."

-- Mary S., 52

Is Natural Hair a No-No for Black Females?

Black Women Object To TSA's Airport Hair Pat Downs

"Some black women who sport natural hairstyles are reporting receiving hair pat downs by the TSA agents at airports even after they've passed full body scans without setting off alarms.

Timery Shante Nance, who's African-American says she doesn't use chemicals or straighteners in her hair. "It's just my natural texture, and I wear it in a normal-looking puff," she told the New York Times."

When a Transportation Security Agency (TSA) official patted her hair in front of everyone, Nance says she felt humiliated, "as if I'd done something wrong."

"Is it just African-American women with natural hair who get the hair search?" Ms. Nance asked the screener because other passengers, including white women with ponytails or bushy hair, were waved through. She filed a complaint but hasn't heard from the agency.

http://colorlines.com/archives/2011/08/black_woman_with_natural_hair_complain_of_hair_pat_downs_by_tsa_at_airports.html

Northern Virginia Hair Care Business Overrun By Racist Posts on Its Facebook Page

ALEXANDRIA, Va. - Racist rants, images and videos are starting to overtake a Facebook page created by a Northern Virginia hair care business with an African American customer base.

One of the owners, Padrica Norfleet of NaturalistaCosmetics.com, told FOX 5's Will Thomas new hate-filled messages appear just as quickly as she deletes the old ones.

The Facebook page is a forum for her customers to discuss hairstyles and offer each other product tips. A video of a KKK cross burning was also posted on her page." (May 9, 2011)

http://www.myfoxdc.com/dpp/news/virginia/northern-virginia-hair-care-business-overrun-by-racist-posts-on-its-facebook-page-050911#ix221fUS2kPnA

***

"If you are a nigger with an amazingly nappy head of velcro, then give *** a shot. Just because you are a nigger, doesn't mean your head has to be greasy like one." (comment posted to the Naturalista Cosmetics Facebook page)

Woman Fired For Cornrows Sues Hyatt Hotel In Virginia

Cheryl Tatum, a cashier, was fired from the Hyatt Regency Hotel in Crystal City, VA, for her refusal to change her "extreme" cornrow hairstyle.

Tatum, a black female, filed a lawsuit against the hotel, charging race discrimination and seeking back pay, punitive damages, and attorney's fees.

Make 'em pay, sista!

Black Corrections Officers Fight 'Extreme' Hair Policy

(2007) Donna Tate-Allison, a guard at Haynesville Correctional Center, was fired for violating the Department of Corrections' grooming policy, which forbids "extreme and eccentric haircuts."

Tate-Allison, a 46-year-old black female, wore her short dreadlocks pinned underneath a hat.

Another black female corrections officer, Juanita Hudson, who wears her hair in cornrows, was informed that "cornrows, dreadlocks, and braids would not be allowed."

After a two-day suspension, one day after receiving a favorable performance review, Hudson took her braids out.

fredericksburg.com/News/
FLS/2007/072007/07022007/295982

Six Flags Denies Jobs to Two Women Based on Natural Hair

(2010) ABC-TV reported a story about two black women who were denied employment at the Six Flags amusement park in Largo, MD, because their locks hairstyle was considered "offensive" by Six Flags management, which does not permit "any hairstyle that detracts or takes away from Six Flags' theme."

One black female job applicant was informed by a supervisor that management was adhering strictly that year to their "grooming policy," in spite of the fact that Largo, MD area is 93 percent black. (April 2010)

SOURCE: www.bvblackspin.com/2010/04/21/six-flags-hair-discrimination-dreadlocks/

'Divorce Court' Judge Mablean Fired -- Cries Racism

(2006) Fox-TV's Divorce Court Judge Mablean Ephriam, was fired after failing to reach an "agreement" over pay and her hairstyle.

According to Ephriam, Fox executives demanded that she wear a wig to "expedite" the hair styling process. Since she was unwilling to agree to the terms, she stepped down after seven years of hosting the successful court show.

Stand your ground, girlfriend!

(2000) FedEx fired several black employees in New York for wearing dreadlocks. Six years later, FedEx reached a settlement agreeing that dreadlocks could be worn for "religious reasons."

Teacher Says She Was Fired Because Of Hairstyle

(2006) Claire Anderson, a Marietta, GA teacher is planning to file a lawsuit after she was fired because her "hairstyle did not fit the image of the school."

Just after she began to wear her hair combed out in a full afro, she was called to the office and fired. (SOURCE: www.wsbtv.cm/news/news/teacher-says-she-was-fired-because-of-hairstyle/nD9mg/

Your 'fro is banging, girl!

Why Do (Some) Whites Find 'Natural Hair' On Black Females So Threatening?

One Answer...

Once the black female stops imitating "white beauty" (white supremacy) and embraces her own GOD-GIVEN natural beauty, her self-respect will skyrocket.

And she will ask herself:

"What other lies have I been taught about myself?"

Once she sheds her former (degraded) self, her NEW EYES will allow her sons and daughters to SEE what has been there all along, right in front of their eyes:

The Majesty Of Their African Ancestors...

And Her Sons...

...will embrace their beloved mother's natural beauty and stop looking elsewhere for the greatness that is already within themselves.

The black male will take her cue, and with NEW EYES, he'll see his own reflection in her natural beauty and...

His self-respect, self-esteem, and sanity will skyrocket as he stops believing the (white) lie, and stops looking outside himself for what is already INSIDE himself.

And that is NOT an acceptable outcome for the black male, black female, and black child in a white supremacy society."

-- Umoja

But Some Sistas Ain't Hearing That And Are Proudly (And Defiantly) Wearing The Naturally Beautiful Hair That The Most High Gave Them...

Cause God Don't Make Junk

"Earlier this month, Emon Fowler launched her Chicago-based "Harriet Experiment," in which she is asking black women to abandon weaves, wigs and chemical relaxers and spend a new year with new hair.

"This is all about breaking free from that hair bondage." -- said Fowler, a black female hairstylist in Chicago, Illinois.

(as reported in Chicago's 'RedEye' newspaper, January 30, 2012)

Some Smart, Savvy Sistas Are Banking The Benjamins They Used To Spend On Hair Relaxers and Hair Weaves...

"Black women spend over $9 BILLION on haircare." -- from the Chris Rock movie, 'Good Hair'

***

According to the 16th annual report on "The Buying Power of Black America" by Target Marketing, a black consumer research firm, blacks spent almost the same amount ($7.4 billion) on hair-care and personal products that we spent on education ($7.5 billion).

Other Sistas Love Not Worrying About "Sweating Their Hair Back" OR Ruining Their Processed "Dos" While Grooming...

***

"When I got my first twists and walked through the door, my huz-band said: WHOA - that's different! After a couple of days, he said: "Baby, I like your hair; it's sexy". [Thank you Baby -- big fat kiss].

He's even sat and watched as I went through the whole grooming process -- and has stated that it's a lot of work, but that my hair looks so much better & healthier, and that he DOES NOT miss seeing my hair (when it was permed) all over the place: sink, tub, floor, here/there.

Bottom line, even though we all want en-couragement from time to time, YOU have to be comfortable with YOU -- both inside & outside."

"Natural Hair Becoming More Popular For African-American Women"

"The number of black women who claim that they don't use chemical relaxers or straighteners has risen to 36% in 2011, which is a significant increase from 26% in 2010. At the same time, sales of relaxers have dropped by 17% over the last five years."

http://blacklikemoi.com/2011/12/health-matters/
natural-hair-popular-african-american-women/

"About time, sista girls!

Let's Not Forget The Brothers Who Love Their Naturally Beautiful Black Women

"Honestly, men who like it, just like it! My boyfriend LOVES it. He said that my hair is so sexy, and he notices that everywhere I go, women are stopping me and asking how I maintain my hair and how long I have been natural.

He feels that more black women need to learn more about their natural hair. His mother has also been natural since he was a child, so he has more of an understanding of it than most black men.

He told me that she had long mid back length hair, and used to allow him to brush it. When he was in high school, she cut it short into a TWA, and he said that she was even more beautiful.

I just LOVE how much he appreciates natural hair for me and my daughter. He says that I am his nappy headed queen." -- Avante, 34

"I'm a black male who loves a black woman with natural hair. I think there is nothing prettier than a woman with dreads, an afro, or anything natural." -- Mike B.

***

For me, natural hair tells me that the sister is smart, confident, and she believes in Afrikan aesthetics and consciousnesss. It also sends the message that she knows who she is, which can be intimidating to a brother who is not comfortable with his own blackness." -- Abdul S.

***

"My boyfriend and I first started dating right after I went natural and I'll admit, I was incredibly nervous about how he felt about it. But I stood tall and remained confident in my hair and in my skin.

A year later and my hair is healthier and growing beautifully (I've also perfected the art of a twist out) and he can be found playing in my hair, conditioning it, or smelling it while I'm in his arms. He loves it and makes a point to tell me that at least 2x a week." -- Nicole

"Don't believe the hype that Black men don't love a woman with natural hair. I can surely attest that I meet a higher caliber of men to choose from than I did before I went natural." -- Shelia W.

***

There is an aura that surrounds a Black woman who wears her hair naturally. Since my girlfriend got rid of her weave and went natural, dudes constantly hit on her at the post office, grocery store, bank, etc. I'm almost tempted to tell her to get a weave just to keep the wolves off. Just kidding!" -- Miles G.

***

"Personally, I MUCH prefer "natural" hair. I also prefer women who are themselves and not trying to jump through hoops to please a man. Changing something fundamental about me in order to attract somebody to me is absurd." -- Freeman

"My Hubby LOVESSSS my hair and he loves it natural and kinky. He has dreads and loves his dreads too, lol.

He DOES NOT care for relaxed straight hair, AT ALL. Never did. He has friends that also dig women with natural hair, too.

I notice that I attract more socially conscious black men now that I wear my hair natural." -- Anna R.

"If I was so ugly and insignificant, the way I wore my hair wouldn't matter to anybody but me. All this hostility tells me there is something about black women loving the body and hair that God gave us that threatens some white people.

Becoming enraged or harassing black females for the way we wear our hair is very revealing. Maybe, they feel wearing our hair natural is the same thing as rejecting white supremacy." -- Avante H.

"Eighty-seven percent of people on kidney dialysis in America are black, even though blacks are only 13 percent of the American population. Black men make up 83 percent of prostate-cancer cases in this country.

Black women are 90 percent more likely to develop thyroid tumors than white women. You know why that is? The beauty parlors.

Beauty parlors are listed as second only to nuclear-waste facilities in the chemical dangers they pose -- and you need a lot more chemicals to straighten out nappy hair than you do blond hair."

-- Dick Gregory, world-famous comedian/author/ social activist/nutrition guru

(SOURCE: 'Cream Rises' by Rose Martelli, Jan 2003 http://www.riverfronttimes.com/2003-01-29/calendar/cream-rises/

Higher Incidence of Secondary Breast Cancer Seen Among Black Women Regardless of Age

When cancer is diagnosed in women younger than 45 years old, the incidence of primary breast cancer is higher among blacks than among whites and the cancer tends to be more aggressive.

"When the disease does occur in blacks early on, it tends to be more aggressive, more likely to be estrogen-receptor negative and it is more likely to cause death," said lead researcher Nsouli-Maktabi Hala, a Ph.D. graduate of The George Washington University." ScienceDaily (Sep. 19, 2011)

http://www.sciencedaily.com/releases/2011/09/110919131605.htm

***

Is There A Link Between Chemically Processed Hair And Breast (And Other) Cancers?

"I am an Afrikan man who loves sisters with natural hair. My love for sisters with natural hair increased when Dick Gregory talked about the link between chemically processed hair and breast cancer. When you think about it, hair chemicals would be an ideal way to poison our women and girl children." - G.B.

A Shout-Out
To All The
Brothers
Rocking
The Naturally
Nappy Hair
The Most High
Gave Them

And those bold, bald brothers the ladies love...

145

STRAIGHT TALK
ABOUT BEAUTY

"Civilized" VS Primitive Beauty Standards

Americans (and other technologically advanced societies) spend billions of dollars to artificially enhance what nature did -- or did not -- give them. Body and face paint, artificially produced suntans, hair weaves, wigs, hairpieces, toupees, hair transplants, makeup, lipstick, eye shadow, hair color, tattoos, piercings, and plastic surgery are used by millions of "civilized" people to make themselves more appealing to the opposite (or the same) sex.

What, then, is the real difference between a woman from the Central African Sara tribe with lip plates and a white woman in Hollywood, California with breast implants (breast plates)? How is the New Zealand Maori warrior with facial tattoos and body markings more "primitive-looking" than the white male college student in Paris, France with body piercings and tattoos?

The westernized Beauty Con Game is a multi-billion-dollar industry that has claimed billions of victims -- of all races -- by creating a false standard of beauty for whites and non-whites.

In order to keep the billions pouring in, the industry must set the bar for "beauty" (normalcy) impossibly high to keep the white and non-white populations insecure. Then, the industry can sell cosmetic "solutions" for imaginary imperfections.

The World's Biggest Beauty Secret

The biggest beauty secret on the planet cannot be found in a $300 vial of skin cream or in a pair of skilled plastic surgeon's hands. What's this secret?

Could it be the infusion of African genes into the European gene pool that gives pale skin more color (and a deeper tan), makes hair thicker, wavy, or curly, and adds more sensuousness (fullness) to lips, noses, and other facial features?

If one studies the history of Africans (Moors), who traveled the ancient world and conquered Europe long before Christopher Columbus sailed to America, one might imagine that "swarthy" (dark) and "olive" complexions, dark, curly, wavy, and wavy-kinky hair; dark hair, dark eyes, and full lips in *some* parts of Europe may be visible evidence of African genetic influences.

While this cannot be stated as scientific fact; it is certainly not an unreasonable theory. If, as scientists have claimed, ALL human life began in Africa -- every man, woman and child is a **modification of the original African man and woman.**

True Beauty Is Not For Sale At The Cosmetic Counter

True beauty is NOT a small, pointy nose, long blond hair, or a pale, bone-thin body. Beauty is the look in a lover's eyes, the curve of a woman's cheek, or a man's broad, strong back. It is a smile that lights up a face, or a laugh that makes us smile. It's the graceful way someone moves or dances. Beauty is eloquence; intelligence; wisdom; kindness; and determination.

God gave all of us something special; a special quality or gift that no one else in the world possesses in the same way we do. God's greatest gifts can be found in a pair of eyes that sparkle, in the hands of a doctor who delivers a new life into the world, or a powerful voice that makes the angels weep. Or it might be the greatest gift of all: a kind, intelligent, loving human being.

Mother Nature Gets The Last Word

Is there a beauty standard that is objective, logical, and can be applied to all human beings, regardless of race? *Absolutely.* Who is qualified to set this standard? The most powerful force on earth: **Mother Nature.**

She is the **PHYSICAL and VISIBLE MANIFESTATION OF GOD**. She is the final judge of all that is good and perfect in this world. Mother Nature does not acknowledge beauty or ugliness based on artificial, manmade standards. She does not put more value on a pair of blue eyes than a pair of brown ones.

Only man and woman, in their endless foolishness, put more value on superficial, useless differences than they do on the value of a human life. The shape of a nose, the color of an eye, or the length of hair is a matter of taste, **NOT proof of racial superiority.** There is NO functional purpose that straight blond hair has that is not also present in dark nappy hair.

Is A Blind Blue Eye Superior To A Brown Eye With 20-20 Vision?

What does Mother Nature consider beautiful? A strong body, limbs without deformities; healthy skin, teeth, vitality, good vision, hearing, and speech are beautiful to nature. But the MOST IMPORTANT TRAIT IN EVERY SPECIES is invisible to the human eye: **THE ABILITY TO REPRODUCE.** Yet, the most fertile woman on the planet – THE BLACK WOMAN – is the most demeaned woman on the planet. Again, the question is:

Could the true emotion that fuels so much contempt for the fertile, full-lipped, full-hipped, curvaceous black female be ENVY? Mother Nature may have already answered that question.

Behind The Mask: The Real Agenda Behind The Beauty Con Game

10

Reasons
Blacks Are
The Main
Targets Of
The Beauty
Con Game

Reason #1

To
"Scientifically"
Prove Blacks
Are Inferior
To Whites

"Why are so many scientific studies focused on putting black females down? If I'm so pitiful, won't that be obvious to everyone without you constantly telling them?

For argument's sake, let's say they're right, that black women are the least attractive. Does that mean I deserve to be mistreated? And if it means that, what does that say about you?

That's like going out in your backyard and stomping on ants. It makes no sense -- unless those ants are a threat to you. Black females must be a threat to white people, otherwise, the media wouldn't keep publishing these articles.

Psychology Today removing the article doesn't mean anything; otherwise, they would have never published it in the first place. They used a non-white person to say what whites have been saying for centuries. It's the good cop, bad cop scenario. Black people must wise up and come up with our own counter-racist strategies."

-- Pamela, 44, blogger

CHAPTER 13

SCIENCE? OR
PSEUDO-SCIENTIFIC BULL?

"Mental health bimonthly Psychology Today came under fire Monday after it published a blog post titled, "Why are African American Women Less Physically Attractive Than Other Women?" by Dr. Satoshi Kanazawa.

In response to the predictably ensuing backlash, the magazine softened the provocative headline by changing it to: "Why are African-American Women Rated Less Attractive Than Other Women, But Black Men Are Rated Better Looking Than Other Men?" (SOURCE: http://racismdaily. com/2011/05/17/psychology-today-draws-ire-for-study-claiming-black-women-are-unattractive/)

It's apparent (to the Authors) that the owners and controllers of the *Psychology Today* publication were FULLY aware of the CONTENTS of the article, and in fact, added more fuel to the fire by **RE-WORDING** the headline to make it sound like a compliment to black males (a divide-and-conquer tactic) *so black males would be less likely to be offended AND less likely to come to the defense of black females.*

A VERY SLICK STRATEGY, INDEED...

Unfortunately, (or fortunately), the article itself was NOT as skillfully (or as cunningly) crafted as the second headline. The author, Kanazawa, using a "third party study," based his "scientific" findings on interviews where the physical attractiveness of an UNNAMED number of respondents (who could be as many as a thousand or as few as two or three in his article) were graded on a scale of 1 to 5 by - in his OWN words -- *"...three different interviewers over seven years."*

Kanazawa then "scientifically" concluded -- **without presenting a shred of SCIENTIFIC evidence** -- that the higher testosterone levels in black women made them more manly, and therefore less pretty.

"The only thing I can think of that might potentially explain the lower average level of physical attractiveness among black women is testosterone. Africans on average have higher levels of testosterone than other races, and testosterone, being an androgen (male hormone), affects the physical attractiveness of men and women differently."

THE ONLY THING HE CAN THINK OF?

Even to the unscientifically trained ear, it certainly sounds like Kanazawa isn't sure himself how to explain WHY (he thinks) black females are less attractive. He completely ignores the WHITE BEAUTY STANDARD that penalizes black AND Asian females -- AND that white females would fare FAR WORSE if they were judged by an (authentically) black OR Asian beauty standard.

He also ignores the FACT that white beauty standards define dark as "masculine." For example, the ideal description of a man for a white female is *"tall, dark, and handsome."*

"Dark" always dominates "light." This may explain why some paler-skinned people are repelled (and INTIMIDATED) by darker-skinned people -- and because of this INSECURITY must INFERIORIZE them.

For the sexually insecure, pale-skinned male, a "darker" female may repel him -- NOT because she is unattractive - but due to his own feelings of COLOR INADEQUACY.

Comparing black females to white females WITHOUT acknowledging that a white beauty standard is at work, is just as illogical as comparing a Great Dane to a Poodle without acknowledging it is NORMAL for different breeds of dogs to LOOK DIFFERENT.

Kanazawa treads into even deeper (and hotter) water by adding that black women have more masculine features because they have higher levels of testosterone than non-black women.

HOWEVER, in the October 2011 issue of *'REPRODUCTION AND ANDROGEN DISORDERS ENDOCRINE TODAY,'* it was reported that: ***"Estrogen Levels Higher Among Black Women During Menstrual Cycle."***

www.cedars-sinai.edu/Patients/Health-Conditions/Uterine-Fibroids.aspx

Another Study Weighs In:

"Study Says Black Women Have Higher Estrogen Than White Women"

"...(after menopause)...African-American women had lower rates of breast cancer than white women did, despite having higher estrogen levels." -- *Dr. Veronica Wendy Setiawan of the University of Southern California, June 5, 2011*

www.dawnali.com/lovinmysistas/index.php?topic=4406.0 - Cached - Similar

This seems to CONTRADICTS Kanawawa's conclusion that black females have higher levels of testosterone than white females.

The Difference Between Estrogen And Testosterone

Testosterone is involved in:

- Development of male sexual organs
- Greater bone density
- Denser hair (on face and chest)

Estrogen is involved in:

- Development of female sexual organs
- Increase in fat tissue around the thighs, hips and breasts
- pregnancy and ovulation

Obviously, black females are NOT more likely to have MALE SEXUAL ORGANS, chest hair, or beards than white females but a good percentage do have "fat tissue" around their curvaceous hips, thighs, and buttocks -- much to the delight of their black (and non-black) male admirers(!)

DOES ESTROGEN AFFECT FEMALE FERTILITY?

ABSOLUTELY. Estrogen is the **dominant hormone** in the first half of the menstrual cycle and continues to play a part throughout the second half as well. If estrogen is low, the lining of the uterus is not hospitable to a pregnancy. *Ovulation may not occur at all.*

The (dark-skinned) AFRICAN FEMALE has **a higher fertility rate** (the total number of children the average woman is likely to have) that ranges from seven or more children -- than the EUROPEAN FEMALE who has **the lowest fertility rate** (around one child per woman). (This *might* indicate that the "testosterone issue" should be more widely explored among the white female than the black female population).

Once we re-examine Kanazawa's "logic" -- that black women (must) have more testosterone because (HE THINKS) they are "less attractive," -- it is obvious that:

KANAZAWA FORGOT ABOUT THE ASIAN "ELEPHANT" IN THE ROOM...

Asian males are often PERCEIVED as LESS masculine (and less attractive) than non-Asian males by WHITE BEAUTY STANDARDS. Should we assume Asian males have MORE ESTROGEN than black and white males?

LOOKS LIKE THE (RACISM) KNIFE CUTS BOTH WAYS

It gets even better

NOT ONLY ARE BLACK WOMEN LESS FEMININE; BEAUTIFUL PEOPLE ARE *MORE* INTELLIGENT

"Beautiful People Really ARE More Intelligent" (Article by Satoshi Kanazawa in the Scientific Fundamentalist - December 12, 2010)

THE FIRST LINE IN THE ARTICLE READS:

"Beautiful people have higher intelligence than ugly people, especially if they are men..."

HE GOES ON TO SAY:

"...more intelligent and higher status men of greater resources marry more beautiful women. Because both intelligence and physical attractiveness are highly heritable, their children will be simultaneously more beautiful and more intelligent."

WONDER HOW ALBERT EINSTEIN WOULD RATE ON KANAZAWA'S "ATTRACTIVENESS" SCALE?

How does Kanazawa define "intelligence?" HE DOESN'T. In addition, studies have shown that attractive people are perceived as more intelligent than people who are considered less "attractive" based on looks alone.

THAT IS NOT SCIENCE, THAT IS IGNORANCE

Kanazawa also claimed that *"higher status men" marry more beautiful women." There is NO scientific evidence to support this statement.*

However, if Kanazawa believes attractive people are MORE intelligent than less attractive people AND that black males are rated more attractive than non-black males, then logically speaking, **black males MUST BE MORE INTELLIGENT than Asian AND white males.**

Not surprisingly, Kanazawa, who described himself as a "scientific purist," *does NOT make that connection in his article.*

Unlike the race "scientists" whose sole purpose seems to be a desperate attempt to prove blacks are inferior, the Authors do not believe Asian males are inherently less masculine OR less intelligent than black or white males.

However, there are exceptions to every rule, especially when NON-WHITES use "racist science" to degrade OTHER NON-WHITES even when they don't meet those white beauty standards themselves.

CHAPTER 14

GOOD COPS/BAD COPS IN THE MAINSTREAM MEDIA

"Good cops/bad cops often come in the following disguises:

- White Democrat VS White Republican.
- White Liberal VS White Conservative.
- White Racist VS White Anti-Racist Activist
- White Segregationist VS White Integrationist

How The "Game" Is Played:

Example 1:

A murder suspect is arrested. During the interrogation, the "bad cop" verbally abuses and physically threatens the suspect. His partner -- the "good cop" – steps in and chastises the good cop for "being too rough" on the suspect, and tells the suspect that he looks like a good guy who wants to help the police by telling what he knows (without benefit of legal counsel) because, *"An innocent man doesn't need a lawyer to tell the truth."*

The suspect – who is actually innocent – is so relieved that the good cop rescued him from the bad cop that he wants to prove he's a "good guy" and winds up talking himself right into a first-degree murder charge.

The two cops are ON THE SAME TEAM, HAVE THE SAME AGENDA, and the same GOAL: *to find a murder suspect to stand trial.*

Example 2:

A prosecutor badgers a key witness for the defense by making obviously false statements (LYING) that incriminates the defendant. The prosecutor knows the defense attorney will "object" and the judge will tell the jury to disregard the testimony.

But the prosecutor also knows the jury can't "un-hear" what they've already heard, just like a bell can't be un-rung. The cunning prosecutor deliberately planted a false "guilty verdict"seed in the minds of the jurors. It's a gamble that may pay off when it's time to render a verdict -- even if that means convicting an innocent man -- *because the prosecutor knows the jury won't forget what they heard*.

GOOD COPS/BAD COPS IN THE MAINSTREAM MEDIA

This "strategy" often takes the form of a controversial comment or a racist article in a mainstream publication, newspaper, or website. For example, a racist article about blacks being less intelligent than whites appears in a mainstream newspaper.

The news media steps in to make sure that this "article" is widely publicized on news broadcasts until the predictable firestorm from outraged black "civil rights leaders" and white liberals occurs. The newspaper suddenly "realizes its "error," issues a formal apology, and the author of the article is fired (AKA temporarily suspended).

HOWEVER

Just like the prosecutor in a trial, the damage has already been done, and the bell cannot be un-rung; nor can the "blacks are less intelligent" message be erased from the minds (or the memories) of the public.

Another Refined Example Of Good Cops/Bad Cops

A mainstream media publication allows (or hires) a non-white person to declare blacks as inferior. The news media broadcasts the racist article all over the planet, while publicly DENOUNCING the article to make it APPEAR that a non-white person is practicing racism *which CANNOT be true because a non-white person cannot be a racist.* (see page 37).

Anymore than the public can erase the most important message contained in that article: blacks are inferior.

As planned AND predicted, the black collective blames the NON-WHITE SCAPEGOAT for the racist article because most do not understand that NOTHING IS PUBLISHED OR BROADCAST in ANY national publication or TV program WITHOUT THE PERMISSION of the (white) people who OWN and CONTROL those media outlets.

The Real Question That Should Be Asked

The question isn't why the article was written or published. That's been established: *white supremacy.* The real question is why is the black female is such a huge threat to the system of white supremacy that it would so vigorously, relentlessly, and BOLDLY attack her BEAUTY and her femininity? The answer may lie in the desperate attempt (and need) to make her appear inferior.

CHAPTER 15

SCIENTIFIC RACISM
IS NOTHING NEW

'Scientific Racism' in its simplest terms means USING SCIENCE to confirm what the "race scientist" already believes OR wants to believe: that blacks and other non-whites are inferior to whites **because they are NOT white.**

The main purpose of "racist science" is to JUSTIFY the mistreatment of non-whites. This explains why the majority of this "scientific research" occurred during the era of slavery, apartheid, and legal segregation.

The Illogical (And Unscientific) Conclusions Of Some Well-Known 'Race Scientists'

Robert Boyle (17th century)

Boyle believed Adam and Eve were originally white and that Caucasians could give birth to different coloured races.

Carl Linnaeus (1739)

Linnaeus believed each race possessed innate characteristics: the Americanus (Native Americans) were red-skinned, of stubborn character, and angered easily; the Africanus (Africans) were black-skinned, relaxed, and of negligent character; the Asiaticus race (Asians) were yellow-skinned, avaricious, and easily distracted; and the Europeanus (Europeans) were white-skinned, of gentle character, and inventive mind.

Benjamin Rush

Rush, a Founding Father of the United States and a physician, said that being black was a hereditary skin disease, which he called "negroidism," and that it could be cured. Rush believed non-whites were really white underneath but they were stricken with a non-contagious form of leprosy which darkened their skin color.

Georges Cuvier (1769–1832)

Cuvier believed there were three distinct races: the Caucasian (white), Mongolian (yellow), and the Ethiopian (black). He thought Adam and Eve were Caucasian, that the Caucasian skull had the most beautiful shape, and judged the quality of civilizations by the beauty or ugliness of their skulls. Some examples of Cuvier's writings:

> "The white race, with oval face, straight hair and nose, to which the civilised people of Europe belong and which appear to us the most beautiful of all, is also superior to others by its genius, courage and activity."

> "The Negro race... is marked by black complexion, crisped of woolly hair, compressed cranium and a flat nose, The projection of the lower parts of the face, and the thick lips, evidently approximate it to the monkey tribe: the hordes of which it consists have always remained in the most complete state of barbarism."

Johan Friedrich Blumenbach (1752 - 1840)

Blumenbach believed in the "degeneration theory" of racial origins; that Adam and Eve were Caucasian; that non-white races originated by degenerative environmental factors, such as the sun and poor dieting; and that Negroid pigmentation was caused by the heat of the tropical sun.

Josiah Clark Nott and George Robins Gliddon (1857)

Claimed "Negroes" were a creational rank between "Greeks" and chimpanzees.

John Hunter (1728–1793)

Hunter claimed that the Negroid race was White at birth but over time the sun turned people "black".

Samuel Stanhope Smith

Smith wrote an essay in 1787 where he claimed that Negro pigmentation was nothing more than a huge freckle that covered the whole body as a result of an oversupply of bile, which was caused by tropical climates.

Ebenezer Sibly

Sibly believed that no humans had reached Africa until after the dispersal from Babel, that the continent's first inhabitants had been white and that Africans had become dark only as a result of the actions of the climate there over successive generations.

Friedrich Hegel (1770–1831)

Hegel declared that, *"Africa is no historical part of the world."* He also claimed that blacks had no *"sense of personality; their spirit sleeps, remains sunk in itself, makes no advance, and thus parallels the compact, undifferentiated mass of the African continent."*

Christoph Meiners (1747–1810)

Meiners split mankind into two divisions: the "beautiful White race" and the "ugly Black race". In his book, 'The Outline of History of Mankind,' he wrote that the main characteristic of race is either beauty or ugliness. He thought only the White race (excluding Slavs) to be beautiful. He considered ugly races to be inferior, immoral, animal-like, and had a "sad" lack of virtue.

He claimed that the Negro felt less pain than any other race and lacked in emotions, due to having 'thick nerves,' was not sensitive like the other races, and had "no human, barely any animal feeling." He described a story where a Negro was condemned to death by being burned alive, and half way through the burning the Negro asked to smoke a pipe, and casually smoked it while being burned alive.

He concluded that Negroes had bigger teeth and jaws than any other race, because they were "all carnivores."He also wrote that the skull of the Negro was larger but the brain of the Negro was smaller than any other race, and that the Negro was the most unhealthy race on earth because of the Negro's poor diet, mode of living, lack of morals, and unduly strong and perverted sex drives.

(Authors' Note: what is amazing is by the same people who had such 'high morals' that they enslaved, raped, and sold other human beings are blaming their slaves (VICTIMS) for having a "...poor diet, mode of living, and lack of morals...(!)"

Ernst Haeckel

Haeckel divided human beings into ten races, with the Caucasian rating the highest while he predicted that the *"primitives were doomed to extinction."*

(Authors' Note: Haeckel's predictions fell far from the mark. According to a 2008 report by the National Policy Institute:

"Global White Population to Plummet to Single Digit—Black Population to Double. As a percentage of world inhabitants the white population will plummet to a single digit (9.76%) by 2060... the big gainer in the population derby will be blacks or sub-Sahara Africans...will expand almost 133% to 2.7 billion by 2060 (25.38% of the world's population). Of the seven population groups studied, only whites are projected to sustain an absolute decline in numbers."

Using Beauty, Intelligence, AND 'Race Science' To Justify Slavery, Oppression, and Genocide

AMERICAN SLAVERY

The Christian Bible was used to justify slavery, and, was often quoted from by writers such as Rev. Richard Furman and Thomas R. Cobb, to enforce the notion that the *physical appearance* of negroes made them suitable for slavery.

In the United States, 'scientific racism' justified Black African slavery and neutralized any moral opposition by portraying blacks as less than human and *"uniquely fitted for bondage."*

Physician Samuel A. Cartwright (1793–1863), considered slave escape attempts to be a mental illness (known as "drapetomania") that *"...with proper medical advice, strictly followed, this troublesome practice that many Negroes have of running away can be almost entirely prevented."*

It was common for Southern slaver-owners to believe (or pretend to believe) that runaway slaves were suffering from *"mental disorders."*

APARTHEID

'Scientific racism' played a major role in establishing the system of Apartheid in South Africa. White scientists, like Dudly Kidd, believed that the cultural differences between whites and blacks in South Africa might be caused by physiological differences in the brain, and described Africans as "hopelessly deficient," yet "very shrewd."

Yet -- a memo sent to Frederick Keppel, then president of the Carnegie Corporation said, "...there was *"little doubt that if the natives were given full economic opportunity, the more competent among them would soon outstrip the less competent whites."*

In other words, poor whites contradicted (exposed the false) notions of racial superiority, and hence it became the focus of "scientific" study. Since poor whites in South Africa had not "overcome" their circumstances any better than the poor (African) "natives," scientific justifications for racism were not as useful in South Africa as they were in the U.S. and Europe.

NAZISM

Herman Lundborg, the director of *Statens Institut För Rasbiologi* in Sweden, was responsible for an eugenics program which attempted to justify the view that European peoples east of Sweden were Asian and thus of inferior race, justifying colonialism and eugenics (forced sterilization). Swedish racism played a major role for the later Nazism in Germany.

EUGENICS (FORCED STERILIZATION OF NON-WHITES)

What is "eugenics?" It is often described as *"improving the genetic composition of a population,"* but in reality it is the use of "scientific racism" to JUSTIFY the STERILIZATION and EXTERMINATION of selected populations by white organizations and/or governments. These "undesirables" also included the disabled, those with genetic defects, the poor, the elderly, the mentally retarded, AND all non-white groups that are considered physically unappealing to "white eyes."

Adolph Hitler (1889-1945)

Hitler believed the German population had been corrupted by the infusion of racially impure (non-white) elements into their bloodstream, and those "elements" (people) should be neutralized *by any means necessary*, while encouraging the "racially pure" (white) people to have more children.

Dr. William Shockley (1910 – 1989)

Shockley claimed the higher rate of reproduction among the less intelligent would ultimately lead to a decline in civilization, and expressed concern that blacks would become progressively less intelligent with time.

'The Bell Curve' -- Richard J. Herrnstein, co-author (1930 -1994)

The Bell Curve, published in 1994, argued that intelligence was largely (40% to 80%) heritable, and that a environmental factors did not affect a person's IQ to any significant degree. The controversial book claimed there was a relationship between anti-social behavior and low African-American test scores. He recommended the elimination of welfare policies that encouraged poor women to have babies.

James D. Watson – (1928 -)

Watson advocated genetic screening and engineering, arguing that stupidity is a disease and the "really stupid" bottom 10% of people should be cured. *"I am inherently gloomy about the prospect of Africa because all our social policies are based on the fact that their intelligence is the same as ours— whereas all the testing says not really."*

The SAME "SCIENCE" used by Hilter to JUSTIFY the slaughter of non-whites is STILL used today to JUSTIFY the final phase of white supremacy:

BLACK AND NON-WHITE MASS GENOCIDE

Britain's Brainiest Family is Black and Has 9-Year-Old High School-Bound Twins

"These precocious London-based tykes, known as the "Wonder Twins," floored academics a year ago when they aced University of Cambridge's advanced mathematics exam. They are the youngest students to ever pass the test." (SOURCE: http://www.bvblackspin.com/2010/03/02/britains-brainiest-family-is-black/

9-year-olds Paula and Peter Imafidon are about to make British history as the youngest children to enter high school.

Their father, Chris, and mother, Ann, immigrated to Britain from Nigeria more than 30 years ago and have three other daughters who are overachievers.

CHAPTER 16

ARE BLACKS (REALLY) LESS INTELLIGENT THAN WHITES?

Let's cut to the chase. Are black people (really) less intelligent genetically than whites?

Absolutely! According to Adolph Hitler, Charles Darwin, Dr. William Shockley (a Nobel Prize Winner in Physics), Richard J. Herrnstein, co-author of the controversial "The Bell Curve," Arthur Jensen, James D. Watson (a Nobel Prize winner in medicine), and many others too numerous to list here.

This "racial superiority" argument has been used for centuries to justify slavery, murder, rape, exploitation, imperialism, and the oppression of non-whites all over the world. It was used to devastate millions via the African and the Jewish Holocausts. Today, this same "science" is used to promote black inferiority/white superiority by ignoring the unequal educational playing field between whites and non-whites.

With a heavy, collective sigh, reasonable (black and non-black) people wonder why (some) whites are so obsessed with the need to be superior. The best answer might be found in the definition of a "superiority complex." According to Alfred Adler (1870 – 1937), one of the most respected psychoanalysts of his time, a *"superiority complex"* is:

"A subconscious neurotic mechanism of compensation developed by the individual as a result of feelings of inferiority."

The theory of "white intellectual superiority" was put to the test during a televised debate between Dr. William Shockley and Dr. Frances Cress Welsing on "Tony Brown's Journal" in 1973. Dr. Frances Cress Welsing, a brilliant, black, medically trained doctor of psychiatry, confidently gutted Dr. Shockley's "theories" on black intellectual inferiority.

Unfortunately for Dr. Shockley, this was done in front of a national audience. He succeeded in debunking his OWN theories of superior white intelligence by losing the debate to a truly superior black intellect – Dr. Welsing's.

Perhaps this very public loss of face explains why Dr. William Shockley disappeared from the national scientific scene after being humiliated on national TV by an "inferior" black female.

Just for argument's sake, let's assume Dr. Shockley is correct when he says blacks are intellectually inferior to whites. That would mean...

EVERY black scientist, geneticist, mathematician, architect, dentist, author, engineer, scholar, doctor, chemist, builder, astronomer, astronaut, inventor, Pulitzer Prize winner, computer engineer, businessman, student, computer programmer, pilot, business owner, electrician, plumber, network engineer, demolition expert, Secretary of State, Supreme Court justice, lawyer, judge, pharmacist, MBA, PhD, and Rhodes Scholar is the intellectual inferior of EVERY white high school dropout because...

...genetic intellectual superiority is a constant.

EVERY elephant is more intelligent than EVERY earthworm, because it is genetically impossible for a less intelligent species (earthworms) to be occasionally more intelligent than a more intelligent species (elephants).

If Charles Darwin, William Shockley, and Adolph Hitler are correct, intellectual superiority is not affected by family income, environment, nutrition, educational background, or a prestigious pre-school. Intellectual superiority does not skip generations, city blocks, or occur randomly.

If genetics is the MAIN factor in determining a person's IQ then the academic performance of a white child from the poorest part of Appalachia should be equal to that of a privileged white child who lives on NYC's Park Avenue and attends private school.

If Richard J. Herrnstein, Charles Murray, and James D. Watson are correct that blacks are intellectually inferior to whites, every poor white high school dropout from rural Appalachia would be the intellectual superior of every black Harvard graduate because...

...genetic intellectual superiority is a constant.

However, if the two things being compared (like black people and white people) are similar enough, measuring the differences between them can be done ONLY IF ALL THINGS ARE EQUAL.

In other words, to accurately compare the intellectual capacity of black children with white children, the white child and the black child must have EQUAL access, EQUAL exposure, EQUAL environments, EQUAL nutrition, and EQUAL cultural affirmations over a set period of time until the effects of any prior disadvantages have been **completely neutralized**.

For example, if two men are betting that each can run the faster race, and one man breaks his leg before the race, the race must be postponed. In order to have a FAIR race to determine which man is the faster runner, the healthy man must wait until the other man fully recovers.

Only then can we fairly and accurately determine WHO is the faster, superior runner of the two. Only by comparing one apple with another apple, can we determine which is the superior piece of fruit.

Fake Science Masquerading As Real Science: Debunking IQ And Standardized Intelligence Tests

Even Alfred Binet (1905), a French psychologist and **the creator of the Binet-Simon intelligence scale** (which IQ tests are based on), did not believe IQ test scales accurately measured intelligence:

"The scale, properly speaking, does not permit the measure of intelligence, because intellectual qualities are not superposable, and therefore cannot be measured as linear surfaces are measured."

In other words, intelligence cannot be measured the same way we would measure a cup of flour.

Binet argued that with proper remedial education programs, most students, regardless of background, could catch up and perform quite well in school. He did not believe that intelligence was a measurable fixed entity. He concluded:

*"We must protest and react against this brutal pessimism (that an individual's intelligence is a fixed quantity); we must try to demonstrate **that it is founded on nothing**."*

Who Tests The IQ Of The IQ Test Makers?

After revising some IQ tests in the 1940's, women began outscoring men, even though women were considered genetically less intelligent than men. In response, the test makers did the "intelligent" thing. They changed the IQ tests until the men were scoring equally.

Some Facts About IQ:

- **Every word in our vocabulary is LEARNED not INHERITED.** The more words spoken around children, the larger the vocabulary. A child who grows up around educated adults will have a larger vocabulary than a child who does not, and will score higher on IQ tests. A large vocabulary is NOT proof of any genetic superiority; but may be proof of a superior (learning) environment.

- Proper maternal childhood nutrition is critical for fetal development. Malnutrition and other environmental factors, such as prenatal exposure to toxins and lead, duration of breast-feeding, the health of the mother and father, and vitamin deficiencies can affect IQ.

- Obviously, poverty, the lack of prenatal care, fresh food, and clean air will affect fetal development. Premature, underweight babies are common among poor, teenage mothers. Fortunately, in many cases, the damage can be reversed if environmental conditions improve.

- A study of French children adopted between the ages of four and six shows the connection between nature and nurture. The children came from poor backgrounds with IQs that initially averaged 77, putting them near retardation. Nine years after adoption, they retook the IQ tests and all the children did better. The amount they improved was directly related to the adopting family's **financial status**.

Some Final Words On Manufactured Intelligence Tests

It is illogical to believe intelligence can be accurately measured by ONE PAPER TEST. It is just as illogical to believe an intelligence test can be completely objective because there isn't a single human being on earth who is capable of complete objectivity or fairness.

Any scientist (with a normal IQ) and a healthy respect for science knows it is **impossible** to measure the effects of nature VS nurture with a single man-made test since intelligence is much more complex than the ability to mark the "best" answer on a sheet of paper.

Those Who Rely On Intelligence Tests May Not Be As Intelligent As They Think

James D. Watson, who believes in white intellectual superiority, also believes stupidity can be and should be cured. We agree wholeheartedly, Mr. Watson.

To end stupidity, we propose starting with those people who believe intellectual superiority can be measured by a paper test -- even when one group has had superior economic, social, and educational opportunities for 400 YEARS that have been DENIED to another group.

Ending stupidity should start with eliminating the (neurotic) NEED to be superior to ANYONE, let alone, everyone of another race. If we could all agree to end the unnecessary (and frankly, embarrassing) "intellectual" debate about "white racial superiority" in a white supremacy society that stacks the deck AGAINST non-whites, perhaps we would have the time and the will to eliminate racism/white supremacy for good.

"If you really understand racism and white supremacy, it's a sign of insecurity. People that are secure, are comfortable with differences.

Only insecure people have to rationalize, because I'm different from you, then I'm better than you. So I don't allow those whites who are racist, who believe in white supremacy, to put their insecurities on me.

If we were inferior, there would be no need to discriminate, which means that the people who are insecure, that believe in racism/white supremacy, they know if African-Americans were given the same opportunities, we would succeed.

-- Dr. Jawanza Kunjufu, educational consultant and author of 'The Conspiracy to Destroy Black Boys'

9

More Reasons Blacks Are The Main Targets Of The Beauty Con Game

If you can control a man's thinking, you don't have to worry about his actions. If you can determine what a man thinks you do not have worry about what he will do.

If you can make a man believe that he is inferior, you don't have to compel him to seek an inferior status, he will do so without being told and if you can make a man believe that he is justly an out-cast, you don't have to order him to the back door, he will go to the back door on his own and if there is no back door, the very nature of the man will demand that you build one."

Carter G. Woodson (1875-1950)

Reason #2: To Reinforce 'The (Manufactured) Black Inferiority Complex'

What is the *"Manufactured Black Inferiority Complex?"* It's the collective self-esteem damage caused by slavery AND post-slavery racism.

This "inferiority complex" is systematically "nurtured" AND reinforced by white society, especially by those in positions of power and influence, who regularly say, write, publish, broadcast, or do racist things that are DELIBERATELY PUBLICIZED to accomplish the following:

1. By PUBLICLY "exposing" racism, this creates the (false) perception that the white mainstream media is opposed to injustice, when in reality, *it is just the opposite.*

2. To **"condition"** blacks to feel angry and HUMILIATED every time a racist article, study, book, scientific 'theory,' cartoon, video, movie, radio or TV show or commercial that degrades a particular black person or blacks in general appears in the media. This public exposure (HUMILIATION) is designed to push the black collective's *"Pavlov's Dog"* buttons to CONDITION us to automatically react in predictable (and desirable) ways.

   The phrase, 'Pavlov's Dog,' describes an experiment where dogs would hear a bell ringing just before they were fed. After a while, the dogs were "conditioned" to associate the sound of a bell with food, and would begin salivating even when no food was present. Like Pavlov's dogs, human beings can be "conditioned" (brainwashed) to react to certain stimuli or situations that are repeated over and over again.

   For example, a cartoon depicting President Barack Obama as a monkey riddled with bullets appears in a national publication. Predictably, blacks are outraged. The 'bad cop' publisher is publicly condemned (but not punished) by the "good cops" in the media. The END RESULT is blacks angry, frustrated, and focused on *non-productive "issues,"* while still firmly attached to our Pavlov's dog "leashes."

3. This ENDLESS REPETITION of racist (black inferiority) messages and images in the media creates a traumatized, demoralized, humiliated, and emotionally exhausted black population, *many of who will seek white validation by ANY means necessary.*

   Those "any means necessary" include appeasing, pleasing, protesting, pleading, clowning, joking, arguing, debating, submitting, integrating, imitating, begging, mimicking, dating, sexing, and breeding with whites -- AND betraying and mistreating other blacks to "prove" (to white people) that we are *"...not like those other blacks."*

Cress Theory of Color Confrontation

Dr. Frances Cress Welsing, a famous African-American psychiatrist and the author of "The Isis Papers: The Keys to the Colors" (1991), states that White Supremacy is practiced by the global "white" minority on the conscious and unconscious level to ensure their genetic survival by any means necessary.

Dr. Welsing contends that because of their "numerical inadequacy" and "color inferiority," white people may have defensively developed "an uncontrollable sense of hostility and aggression" towards people of color, which has led to "confrontations" between the races throughout history.

Repressing their own feelings of inadequacy, whites "set about evolving a social, political, and economic structure to give blacks and other 'non-whites' the appearance of being inferior."

Reason #3: Provides A "Soothing Lotion" For The 'Color Inadequacy Complex' Among The White Collective

"The guys will be mad if we don't show up with a tan." – two white females talking on a TV reality show about their (white) boyfriends.

It is undeniable that the same people who created plastic surgery and tanning salons are not content with their own appearance. Also, the obsessive NEED to classify blacks and non-whites as "inferior" to white is a huge sign of insecurity and low-self-esteem among the white collective.

The negative stereotyping and degrading images of blacks provides a "soothing lotion" for the massive color inferiority complex among the white collective -- OTHERWISE -- these RACIST images and messages would NOT exist -- NOR would they be so widely embraced by whites in general.

Common sense tells us that any people who mistreat people BECAUSE they have "color" then risk their own health (and lives) to get a "tan" (color); and spend millions on cosmetics to give pale skin more "color;" and who AGGRESSIVELY pursue sex with the same people (of color) they despise **are revealing a "burning" desire to HAVE and to EXPERIENCE "color."**

"The white personality, in the presence of color, can be stabilized only by keeping Blacks and other non-whites in obviously inferior positions. The situation of mass proximity to Blacks is intolerable to whites because Blacks are inherently more than equal.

People of color will always have something highly visible that whites never can have or produce — the genetic factor of color. Always, in the presence of color, whites will feel genetically inferior...they can compensate for their color inadequacy only by placing themselves in socially superior positions."

-- Dr. Frances Cress Welsing, of 'The Isis Papers:

Complexions

An essay by America's favorite author, Mark Twain, author of 'The Adventures of Tom Sawyer' (1835-1910)

Nearly all black and brown skins are beautiful, but a beautiful white skin is rare. Where dark complexions are massed, they make the whites look bleached-out, unwholesome, and sometimes frankly ghastly. I could notice this as a boy, down South in the slavery days before the war. The splendid black satin skin of the South African Zulus of Durban seemed to me to come very close to perfection...

The white man's complexion makes no concealments. It can't. It seemed to have been designed as a catch-all for everything that can damage it. Ladies have to paint it, and powder it, and cosmetic it, and diet it with arsenic, and enamel it, and be always enticing it, and persuading it, and pestering it, and fussing at it, to make it beautiful; and they do not succeed.

But these efforts show what they think of the natural complexion, as distributed. As distributed it needs these helps. The complexion which they try to counterfeit is one which nature restricts to the few--to the very few. To ninety-nine persons she gives a bad complexion, to the hundredth a good one. The hundredth can keep it--how long? Ten years, perhaps.

The advantage is with the Zulu, I think. He starts with a beautiful complexion, and it will last him through. And as for the Indian brown--firm, smooth, blemishless, pleasant, and restful to the eye, afraid of no color, harmonizing with all colors and adding a grace to them all--I think there is no sort of chance for the average white complexion against that rich and perfect tint.

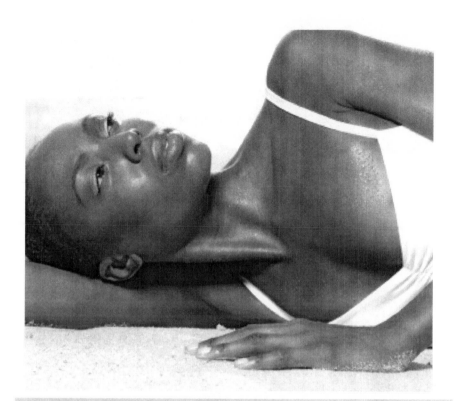

Mark Twain Is Not Alone In His Opinion About The Superior Beauty Of Darker Skin

2,000 women were polled about beauty preferences and 70% of those who wish to change their skin color wanted it to be darker -- especially among (white) women.

(Source: Allure Magazine, March 2011)

An African Novelist Writes About The Beauty of His Women...

"She was slender as a fale stalk, and suppler. From her forehead to her feet her body was of a deep, even blackness that could cause the chance looker to wonder how it was that even the surface of a person's skin could speak of depths.

Her grace was easy in the dance. In the work of every initiation she was skilled enough to have chosen to be a fundi. Men not commonly known for their lechery grew itchy-eyed looking at her."

from the novel, "Two Thousand Seasons" by Ayi Kwei Armah (published 1973)

(A "fundi" is an expert in a particular field)

Framing: Creating Easy Sexual Access

"Every week there's a new study or article that says black women are inferior. Here's the deal.

They have a name for it in the PUA comunity, it's called 'framing.' PUA stands for pick-up artists.

By constantly advertising the idea that black women are at the bottom of the sexual attractiveness heap and saying nobody wants them, they become MUCH easier to get because they feel "lucky" that anyone wants them. This is really a strategy designed to produce easy sexual access to black women for white males.

I once moved into a group house years ago and it took almost six months before it finally hit me that the black female and white male were f*cking. They were so good at keeping it discrete (the white male's choice, no doubt).

If a white male wants to have sex with a black female she should FORCE him to be VISIBLE WITH HER. That means public displays of affection, meeting white mom and dad. Otherwise, she is being treated like a prostitute." J.W. -- black male blogger, 45

Reason #4: "Framing" -- Creating Easy, Unlimited Sexual Access To Black Males And Females

The *"Manufactured Black Inferiority Complex"* creates an unquenchable thirst for white validation -- and provides easy, unlimited sexual access to demoralized black males and females -- even for whites who are openly racist.

What is more "validating" than having sex with the same people who have the POWER to give OR withhold that validation?

Racism and sexual intercourse between blacks and whites operate in tandem, *not in opposition.* Sexual intercourse between blacks and whites UNDER the system of white supremacy is MAXIMUM RACIST AGGRESSION because the confused (black) victims do not understand that having sex with the same people who are oppressing them is literally SLEEPING WITH THEIR ENEMIES -- and deepening their own psychological oppression.

The vast majority of sexual activity between blacks and whites is INITIATED BY WHITES. Blacks do not have the power to coerce whites to fulfill their sexual whims or fantasies -- but whites often use their more powerful social/ economic positions to coerce (MANIPULATE) blacks into complying with their sexual demands. *(Our third book – 'The Interracial Con Game' by Umoja – explores this subject in much greater detail).*

Reason #5: To Neutralize The Black Male

The white media "inferiorizes" the black female WHILE promoting the "superior" white female who will seduce the black male, distract him, remove him from his community, and neutralize his will AND his ability to overcome his oppression. The men of a community are always viewed as the biggest potential threat to their enemies and are "disabled" at the earliest possible age.

Bottom line, you cannot lay down with white supremacy at night and get up in the morning and fight it.

Reason #6: To Eliminate The Possibility Of Black Unity

Since **Black Unity** is the BIGGEST THREAT to white supremacy, the black male and black female are deliberately driven apart by media-generated negative stereotypes and images; the promotion of interracial sex; AND by creating social, educational, economic, and political conditions that create DSYFUNCTION and ANTI-BLACKNESS within the black collective.

You cannot unify with those you have been taught to despise.

"Global White Population to Plummet To Single Digit—Black Population To Double"

As a percentage of world inhabitants the white population will plummet to a single digit (9.76%) by 2060...the big gainer in the population derby will be blacks or sub-Sahara Africans...will expand almost 133% to 2.7 billion by 2060 (25.38% of the world's population).

Of the seven population groups studied, only whites are projected to sustain an absolute decline in numbers." -- 2008 report by the National Policy Institute.

***

"Europe is depopulating itself at a rate unseen since the Black Death of the fourteenth century." - 'Is Europe Dying? Notes on a Crisis of Civilizational Morale' by George Weigel, History News Network, Aug 05)

Reason #7: Economics

The 'Manufactured Black Inferiority Complex' = billions of dollars spent on skin and hair care, jewelry, expensive cars, liquor, designer clothing and shoes, and homes -- all of which saps the wealth potential of the black collective *while enriching those who hold us in contempt.*

Reason #8: Fear Of White Genetic Annihilation

Three of the methods being employed to address the growing infertility and decreasing birth rates of whites all over the world:

1. promoting sex with whites to discourage black males and females from reproducing with each other and increasing the black populations

2. encouraging black males to breed with white females to enhance white genetics with the HIGHER FERTILITY of melanated blacks. The majority of black male/white female "unions" do not last, which means their offspring will be raised by white females; will be more white-identified; and will be more likely to breed with whites. Overall, the creation of a *"new (more melanated) white race"* is hoped to lead to more fertility in future white generations.

3. promoting more homosexuality among black males discourages reproduction with black females AND makes more black males sexually available to openly (or secretly) homosexual white males.

Reason #9: To Set The Stage For Black Genocide

Establishing the (false) INFERIORITY of blacks in appearance, morality, and intelligence reduces the VALUE of ALL black life AND justifies the oppression, sterilization, incarceration, and ultimately, the GENOCIDE of black and African people all over the world.

In addition, the *Manfactured Black Inferiority Complex* reduces the chances that blacks will come together to defend each other OR to defend ourselves when our enemies attack us. The reason is simple: *If we do not respect ourselves, we will NOT protect ourselves.*

*   *"Depopulation should be the highest priority of foreign policy towards the third world." -- Henry Kissinger, 1974*

*   *In the 1970s, South Africa developed race-specific bio-weapons to target blacks and Asians.*

*   *In September 2000, the Project for a New American Century published a document in which Dick Cheney described race-specific bioweapons as "politically useful tools."*

Big in Romania: 'Black Man' Cookies

Big in Romania: 'Black Man' Cookies "You know what I could go for?" said one Romanian to the other. "A 'Black Man' chocolate-flavored cookie. Looks like a black man, tastes like a cookie." Replied the other Romanian, "Here."

According to The Root:

"A report that Romania is selling "Black Man" chocolate-flavored cookies. Based on a photo posted in Copyranter, the cookie appears to have coarse hair, closed eyes, a wide nose, and big lips. It is sporting a Superman cape with a "B" inscribed on a plate in the front."

http://www.theroot.com/buzz/big-romania-black-man-cookies?wpisrc=root_more_news

Reason #10: For The Sheer Enjoyment Of It

The ONLY way white supremacy could have existed for as long as it has existed (over 500 years) *is white supremacists WORLDWIDE really enjoy their work and have NO INTENTION of stopping.*

Part of that "work" is degrading black (and non-white) people because of *their sociopathic NEED to feel superior.*

This may explains the enormous popularity of racist white shock jocks and the huge arsenal of ethnic jokes and stereotypes about non-whites in white culture. In contrast, non-whites spend very little time creating "ethnic" humor, perhaps because too much of their time is spent DEFENDING themselves against it.

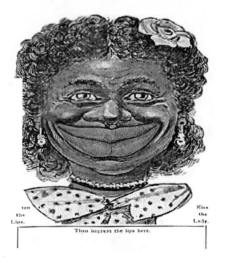

Breaking The Chains Of White Validation

"The language is anti-black, every aspect of white people's system reinforces that anti-blackness. The language talks about how ugly and black, the language makes it seem natural that they go together.

If you look at the terms...when you are in an environment where words are used in a way to constantly denigrate darkness and to uplift, deify, praise whiteness, it's gonna really become instinctual.

When everyone is using words in a manner that reinforces anti-blackness, and it's really something you have to be on the ball about."

-- Gus Renegade, host of C.O.W.S. (www.contextofwhitesupremacy.com)

CHAPTER 17

WHAT IS WHITE VALIDATION

White validation in a white supremacy system can be compared to paper money in a paper-currency financial system where that paper is the STANDARD for buying and selling labor, goods, and services.

"Whiteness" is the STANDARD social "currency." The "whiter" a person is in appearance, speech, behavior, the more valuable their personal "currency" becomes. Blacks seeking white validation in a white supremacy system is as common as poor people seeking money or an injured person seeking medical care. If they were not deprived (poor, injured, or mistreated) *they would NOT NEED what they were "seeking."*

The White-Identified Black

A **white-identified black person** views the world through a white perspective ('white eyes') even when that perspective conflicts with his or her own self AND group interests. The white-identified black person often pursues people, places, activities, and relationships primarily *because white people are associated with them* – and avoids or looks down on certain people, places, and things primarily *because black people are associated with them.*

White-identified blacks can be found anywhere, at every income level, from the most exclusive gated community or Ivy League campus, to an inner-city housing project. How a black person sees black people, talks about black people, treats black people, feels about being black, and treats white people determines the degree of white-identification.

White Supremacy Is The Foundation For White Validation AND White Identification For Blacks (And Non-Whites)

The white supremacy system is based on the following beliefs:

- white is superior to non-white
- whites are more attractive than non-whites
- whites are more intelligent than non-whites
- white people created everything worth creating
- white life is more valuable than non-white life
- white is the most normal (the standard) for ALL human beings

If white is considered the **most normal**, black must be the **most abnormal**. For those who doubt this white standard exists, there is one INDISPUTABLE piece of evidence that can be found in every medicine cabinet in America: **the 'flesh-colored' Band-Aid.**

In other words, the "normal" color for human flesh is the color closest to the skin color of white people. What does this say to the non-white person? That their skin color is NOT normal because they are NOT as human as white people.

The white-identified black who believes "white" is the most normal, most attractive, and most desirable is -- LOGICALLY SPEAKING -- anti-black and ANTI-BLACK-SELF.

TV & Movies PROGRAM Blacks To Seek White Validation

Watching television and Hollywood-produced films are the equivalent of OVERDOSING on white values, white beauty, and white people (white crack) AND programs the young (and not so young) black MIND to see the world via the *white is normal/white is superior viewpoint.*

If you doubt this, think about this: The VAST majority of people in TV shows, commercials and movies are white. All the news and information you receive is from the white perspective even when a black (or non-white) person is the TV anchor or host, politician, or political spokesman.

Anyone AND everyone who is doing anything or saying anything worth doing or saying is usually white. All beauty products advertised are created to enhance "white beauty," and the majority of expressions of romantic love, sex, and affection mainly involve white people.

Black people are seldom shown doing much more than committing crimes, cursing, fighting, singing, joking, clowning, dancing, or acting like buffoons.

White-Identified Blackness = Psychological Suicide

By viewing the world through "white eyes," **white-identified blacks** are in the unenviable position of embracing their own inferiority. If the **white-identified black** is observed interacting with whites or with blacks, he or she will eventually reveal their OWN racial bias and inferiority complexes by the things they say or do.

Their confusion comes from trying to straddle the precarious line between the black world and the white world by serving two opposing masters at the same time: *white supremacy and black normalcy.*

It is unnatural and perverted for a group of people to adopt a perspective and a set of standards that does NOT benefit their group AND denies their own NORMALCY and self-worth as members of that group.

Unfortunately, this kind of distorted thinking is exactly what has led to the personality disorders and self-hatred issues that plague the black population.

White-Identification Leads To Anti-Blackness

By accepting the (false) premise that white is the most 'normal,' the white-identified/white-validation-seeking black person is confirming his or her own black inferiority -- and the inferiority of other black people.

In a white supremacy system "whiteness" is the norm and "blackness" is the disease. Because blacks will NEVER be white, they often spend a lifetime – in vain – seeking the white validation (they will NEVER get).

This confusion leads many blacks to see other blacks through condemning "white eyes" (the way whites see blacks), and will often refer to OTHER blacks as -- "they," "them," "those blacks," "niggers," and other derogatory and ANTI-BLACK terms -- forgetting THEY ARE BLACK and are JUDGED by those same racist stereotypes.

Some blacks attempt to separate themselves from the black masses by mimicking white behavior or socializing exclusively with white people. One of the most destructive (and obvious) forms of white-validation-seeking is the black or non-white person who **deliberately** breeds with a white person to rid their own offspring of the racial 'abnormalities' (blackness) that exist within themselves.

This is the ULTIMATE statement of black self-hatred and "anti-blackness." There is no way we can SAY (or believe that) we love OR respect ourselves and at the same time want to breed our genetics out of existence.

The **white-identified/white-validation-seeking black** is the ADULT VICTIM of the 'Black Doll/White Doll Experiment.' White-identified blacks understand how tragic it is for the little black girl or boy to pick the white doll as the nicer doll, but cannot see how damaged they must be to do the **SAME THING.**

This is NOT a condemnation of the black VICTIMS of white supremacy. ALL blacks are white-identified to some degree because we are programmed to believe white is superior **24-7, 365 days a year from cradle to grave.**

"...blacks should honestly be thankful that whites have brought them into white regions of the world because if it wasn't for that, blacks in all likelihood, would still be in Africa, running around naked, eating themselves and each other while killing each other, raping each other."

-- Joe Adams, admitted white racist, from www.savethewhitepeople.com during an interview on C.O.W.S., Dec 11, 2011

(program available for download in archives of website: contextofwhitesupremacy.com

CHAPTER 18

CONVINCING WHITES THAT BLACKS ARE NOT INFERIOR IS A WASTE OF TIME

During the interview of Joe Adam, a young white male, (see opposite page) outraged (black) listeners attempted to "educate" (CONVINCE) him that blacks have produced much more than a written alphabet.

However, their black history lessons fell on deaf ears. Joe -- an admitted white racist -- could have cared less about 'black inventors' or what blacks had or had not accomplished. On his website, www.savethewhitepeople. com, Joe writes:

"We recognize flat out that the races are natural enemies or natural competitors at least...this really isn't a win-win situation at all. It is win-lose, and we want the White Race to be the winners in the game..."

"The ultimate penalty in Nature's realm is extinction, and the White Race is going that path for failure to obey Nature's laws...The White Race has by far the most to lose. The White Race is Nature's Elite. The White Race is the Creator of all civilization and the Creator of all the great and worthwhile values that have been produced in the last several thousand years. We must save ourselves. No one else will."

Joe is NOT alone. In fact, his views are reflected in the attitudes AND behaviors of whites collectively all over the planet. If Joe represented only a minority of whites, America's racist white shock jocks would not be so plentiful, so well-paid, or so popular with their white audiences.

White people, collectively, DO NOT CARE about the TRUTH of what is being said, written, or broadcast about black people as long as the FOCUS stays on *"what is wrong with black people"* and the PRESSURE keeps black people on the self-defeating treadmill of proving (CONVINCING) whites that blacks are not inferior.

The SMARTEST (and most REFINED) white supremacists are MORE KNOWLEDGEABLE about African/black history than the MAJORITY of black people -- YET this "knowledge" DID NOT STOP them from practicing racism.

"All Prejudice Isn't Created Equal; Whites Distribute It Unequally To Minorities

"A series of six studies conducted by University of Washington and Michigan State University psychologists shows that whites react more negatively to racial minority individuals who strongly identify with their racial group than to racial minority individuals who weakly identify with their group.

The research, published in the current issue of the Journal of Personality and Social Psychology, provides an explanation for why some Blacks report personally experiencing more prejudice than others." (ScienceDaily, Feb. 25, 2009)

http://www.sciencedaily.com/releases/2009/02/090225132241.htm#.TxUmdM5nFhg.email

White Supremacy Is A 'Bully System'

Sam, a freshman in high school, is bullied by Tom, a sophomore, who makes fun of Sam's hair and clothes, even the way he walks and talks. Sam, who was well-liked in grammar school, suddenly becomes self-conscious and insecure.

The younger boy tries to be friendly to Tom, but his attempts are rebuffed. Even after Sam changes the way he dresses and styles his hair to be more like the older boy, he finds his efforts are in vain.

There is nothing wrong with Sam, but he desperately wants the approval (validation) of the BULLY because he is convinced he needs it. Sam has given up his power to Tom who gets off on taking it.

Sam is not the one with the self-esteem problem. Tom is pretending to be "superior" to Sam by projecting his OWN INSECURITIES and LOW-SELF-ESTEEM onto a more vulnerable target (Sam) *to make himself feel better about himself.*

Over the summer, Sam grows two inches and works out. The following year he is asked to join the varsity football team, and his popularity with the other students -- especially the girls -- soars.

Sam no longer needs OR wants Tom's approval because he learned to VALIDATE HIMSELF by his accomplishments.. Looking back, Sam realizes Tom was the one with the self-esteem problem, and has learned a valuable LIFE lesson about the LIE of "superiority complexes."

A Superiority Complex = A FEAR Of Being Inferior

According to Alfred Adler, the founder of the school of individual psychology, a **superiority complex** "*...involves covering up our inferiority by pretending to be superior.*" That being said, if whites collectively TRULY believed blacks were inferior, why would blacks be seen as such a threat?

Why are black females who embrace their own natural beauty being attacked in the media, airports, and workplace? Why are blacks who are smart and confident (like First Lady Michelle Obama) often labeled by whites (like Rush Limbaugh) as "uppity?" Why are images of blacks who express love and sexual interest in other blacks FORBIDDEN in Hollywood movies and television shows?

Because this behavior IS OUT OF SYNC with the Manufactured Black Inferiority Complex, which is ABSOLUTELY NECESSARY to maintain the system of white supremacy.

Whites, collectively, NEED to believe blacks are inferior to JUSTIFY the mistreatment of blacks; to JUSTIFY white privileges; and to VALIDATE "whiteness" to compensate for their OWN inferiority complexes.

"It reminds me of what I heard about George Wallace, who was the Alabama governor some time ago, and Wallace said when he went into politics as a southern white man that he thought that the best thing for poor white people would be for them to unite with black people who were also poor, and they would have political power in that way.

And he said he found out that white people didn't care if they didn't have hospitals, if they didn't have schools, if they didn't have roads, that the thing that was most important to them was to feel like they were better than, superior to, black people.

Now, those feelings are to feel superior to, to feel better than, or I don't want blacks to have the same thing that whites have, I say that those are all expressions of "if the blacks are in positions of equality, then we can be genetically annihilated."

— Dr. Frances C. Welsing during an interview on the COWS internet program, 11/28/2011

Why Whites Will NEVER Validate Blacks

Why would whites collectively -- who depend on a white supremacy system that guarantees MORE privileges for those people classified as "white" -- voluntarily END that system? This is a logical question all blacks should ask themselves:

Any group of people who CREATES an immoral system that justifies mistreating people on the basis of COLOR cannot be trusted to dismantle that system. Any group that BENEFITS UNFAIRLY from the same system they CREATED knows it is NOT in their best interests to reveal the TRUTH about that SYSTEM to the group that is being VICTIMIZED.

It is crucial that non-whites understand that the system of white supremacy will NEVER be dismantled by those who created it, who depend upon it, and who benefit from it.

No amount of begging, crying, pleading, marching, protesting, threatening, boycotting, tantrum-throwing, assimilating, integrating, self-hating, interracial dating, breeding, or marrying will eliminate racism/white supremacy -- because *validating blacks would mean the END of white privileges and white domination over blacks.*

"(White) People everywhere are looking for what I offer. Most won't agree with me openly, but if you ask them privately, they'd tell you, 'Rockwell has the right idea. White Christian people should dominate.'"

-- George Lincoln Rockwell Founder of the American Nazi Party, The Playboy Interview - April 1966
http://www.playboy.com/arts-entertainment/features/george-lincoln-rockwell/george-lincoln-rockwell-02.html

"I disagree as I have seen no evidence to support white people when exposed to non-white people from an early age will not maintain and practice white supremacy.

"To my knowledge black females were used in early America to care for white offspring, even breastfeeding the white children, but unfortunately black people were still grossly mistreated.

"Also I believe white people who are able to interact with nonwhites from an early age, become better equipped to "keep their enemies close" as per art of war and more effectively practice white supremacy."

-- Robert L. Williams, Ph. D., author of 'Racism Learned at an Early Age.' Dr. Williams was interviewed Nov. 17, 2009 by Gus Renegade on The C.O.W.S. Internet Radio Program

CHAPTER 19

THE SINGLE MOST IMPORTANT QUESTION BLACKS SHOULD ASK WHITES

While the Authors would like to take credit for this profound revelation, we admit we borrowed some wisdom from Josh Wickett and his counter-racist review of *"The Matrix"* (www.thecode.net/features/movies/thematrix.htm)

"Counter racism code is based on logic. You follow the logic...no matter where it leads. How do you do that? By using two main tools:

1. Asking question that reveal truth
2. Refusing to lie to yourself or any other people

"Now what is the constructive value of refusing to lie to yourself? It is the key component to the revelation of truth; it's really the only weapon you have against the masters of deception. I no longer engage in those endless discussions regarding how "great" Black people are. The White supremacists trick us into trying to prove to them that we are worthy of not being mistreated.

"I don't try to prove Jesus was Black. I don't run and get my book, "100 inventions by Blaxx"... I pull a "pincer movement" by using words to force the conversation to a point where suggestions must be made—"I'm a stupid nigger, my IQ is the same as my shoe size, I'm an alcoholic, unemployed, HIV positive, I stink, got no money, no job, and one toof, and I look like a monkey, a monkey with one toof! Got it? Now, what do YOU suggest WE do about ME?

"I take it straight there and I don't stop for gas. I'm back-burning. Lay it all out and then wait for their CONSTRUCTIVE suggestion. I often use this technique when a White person starts quoting "Guns Germs and Steel" or talking about what their ancestors did ... I'm like, "wake me up when you get to the part that justifies mistreating people."

Don't be surprised if all you get is silence. You don't need anybody misleading you. You're already a victim of racism. You want to engineer a situation where White people are either making true statements, OR SHUTTIN THA FUCK UP! Its times like these I realize that silence is truly golden and not just yella."

***

"White people will try to get black people in a long debate to prove what we've accomplished and that we're not inferior. None of that is necessary. Just get to the part about mistreatment.

Regardless of what black people have or haven't done, should we be mistreated because we're not white? I've seen white people extend conversations for days trying to prove that black people are inferior.

Rosa Parks didn't give them the history of buses and black people...she just focused on producing justice." – Gus Renegade, host of the internet talk-show, C.O.W.S. – www. contextofwhitesupremacy.com."

– Gus Renegade, host of the C.O.W.S. internet program, 11/28/2011

RACE, EVOLUTION and BEHAVIOR
By J Philippe Rushton

A Counter Racist Book Review by Josh Wickett
(Reprinted with permission)
(www.thecode.net/books/raceevolution_review.htm)

Philippe Rushton is a White male Canadian who has attempted to write about race in an objective manner by using a lot of scientific data and evolutionary theory. Why is this book important for the counter-racist scientist?

Because this is the angle a lot of White people are going to come at you with when you discuss racism with them. They are going to throw facts at you. They are going to hit you with the "mountain of evidence." And this book is full of it (no pun intended).

In "Race, Evolution and Behavior" Rushton divides all people into three groups, Orientals, Whites and Blacks and from there proceeds to show data in areas such as brain size, IQ testing, skeletal development,marital stability, genital size and about 100 other categories to prove that Black people are inferior and have less ability than White people. But in a novel twist, he places Orientals ahead of even White people in terms of intelligence, ability and all the other categories he has invented.

Probably his most controversial theory is in regard to his "r-K" scale of reproductive strategies. It goes like this: White people, Dolphins, Whales, Elephants (all the smart animals) have low fertility and a lower number of offspring which they spend a higher amount of time and energy nurturing and raising, this is the "K" selected reproductive strategy.

On the other hand niggers, clams, fish and rats...(all the lower animals) have a large number of children and just don't take care of them because enough will survive out of the millions they have. This he terms the "r" selected reproductive strategy.

Now I say that when you engage fact-driven White people like this in discussions about race, don't even bother to try and counter their facts and scientific data with facts of your own. Don't go into all that *"we built the pyramids...we were kings and queens in Africa stuff."* You wanna fast forward their argument to get to their motive for bringing this "mountain of evidence" of Black inferiority to the table.

What I do is this, I say:

"Ok, I have a low IQ, I'm HIV positive, I'm unemployed. I'm an alcoholic, I'm a crack head, I have pus filled bleeding gums, I stink, and...I LOOK LIKE A MONKEY!"

"Now, What are WE gonna do about ME?"

This is what you gotta do, just get it all out there for the sake of argument. See White people have tricked us into thinking that we gotta justify NOT being mistreated by them. That we hafta somehow prove ourselves worthy of being treated correctly, as if we could do this in a system of White Supremacy.

If that's the case, you better lock your children up because a 5-year-old is not as smart as the average nigger! Do they deserve to be mistreated? Armed with all the data on Black inferiority that Rushton brings to the table (and it's a lot), White people really only have 3 choices:

1. **Do nothing**
2. **Kill all the niggers**
3. **Help them**

That's basically it. For all of his data, those are his only options (he conveniently leaves this part out of the book, I suspect it's filed under the title, 'What White people talk about when there are no Black people around?') This book is packed with a lot of interesting data, for example, is it just me, or does it seem like a lot of Black guys have deep voices?

Rushton argues that this phenomenon and the other secondary male sexual characteristics are a product of higher levels of testosterone in Black males. Has this subject been addressed anywhere else?

Rushton's most creative racial twist is to place "Orientals" at the top of the racial order with Blacks at the bottom and Whites in the middle. Following that logic he also relates penis size to intelligence with Blacks being well endowed but stupid and "Orientals" being smart with meager members.

Just like in Goldilocks and the three bears, Whites are "just right." Some of you will be amazed at all of the data about race that has been collected, whether its true of not, remember to focus on the motive. Don't get caught up trading facts about race with a White person, I sometimes think they make them up on their lunch hour. And even if every nigger went out and built a pyramid tomorrow, do you think White people would stop practicing racism?

Once White people get you tricked into trying to prove you are worthy of being treated correctly based on some test they invented...JUST FOR YOU! Its all over, you better pack a lunch cause it never ends. I may be a nigger, I may not be smart, but I cannot agree to be mistreated based on my own limitations, especially limitations placed on me by people smarter and more powerful than myself.

Check this book out, its got just about every argument against Black people except the one that justifies mistreating you.

Josh Wickett
RWSWJ (Replace White Supremacy With Justice)

"We know what we've done to (non-whites). And we know what we've put in your head over 500 years. We know how to utilize that. We know how to take advantage of that. We even know how to have a (non-white) black friend.

We know the dynamics of who is in control. We know where your place is. We know where our place is. The greatest deception we caused is that your people believe us. I have done such a good job, they don't even know that I"ve done this to them."

-- Ferrell Winfree, white female, admitted Racist/white Supremacist, on The C.O.W.S Internet Radio Program (2009)

"Nigger" According To Mr. Neely Fuller, Jr.

"A nigger is a non-white person who is subject to white supremacy. That's the truth. So, people have asked me, 'Do I fit that description?' I say yes, but now, everything in the codebook is supposed to be of constructive value. Otherwise, it's not supposed to be in there.

So, a person may ask how is that constructive, for a white person to call you a nigger and you admit that you are one? You give the definition. Now what have you done when you say the definition of me being a nigger is that I am subject to white supremacy.

Now, what you are doing is indicting the white people who are white supremacists. You have taken the word and made it an indictment, not of yourself, but just of a description of yourself because of what is being done to you.

And then I elaborate on the word 'nigger' by taking it further so people get a dimension of the implications for the word. I call it when a black person is taken under white supremacy and taken through the process of 'niggerization.'

To end this process you have to end white supremacy through codification and that is the process of de-niggerization. If you're looking for a word that's equivalent to the word 'nigger' as applied to a non-white person, it just means a prisoner of injustice."

CHAPTER 20

SEVEN SUGGESTIONS FOR INCREASING BLACK-SELF-VALIDATION

#1: -- Take Control Of The Words Used Against Us

WHAT IF...

...we took the POSITION that "nappy" hair was "good" hair? What if the next time someone said our hair was "nappy" our response was to SMILE and say, *"Thanks! I love my nappy hair, too!"*

Because you realized there was nothing WRONG with the hair that GOD gave you, and in fact, you actually LIKED your hair because it was growing out of YOUR head and your woman or man liked your natural hair because it looked identical to the hair growing out of their heads, and nappy was no longer a bad word even if there were other, better words to describe the "crowning glory" the MOST HIGH had blessed you with.

What would be the most likely response of a person who wanted to insult you by calling your hair "nappy?"

To stop calling "nappy" hair "nappy."

Because it is IMPOSSIBLE to insult someone by calling them something OR saying something they don't think is an INSULT.

WHAT IF...

...the word "nigger" described the CREATOR of the word instead of describing the TARGET of the word (black people)?

What if ALL black people deferred to the wisdom of Mr. Neely Fuller, Jr. (seen on the opposite page) when he defines the word *"nigger?"*

Because once we understand what a "nigger" is, we will understand that a made-up word **DOES NOT DEFINE WHO WE ARE; it defines WHAT IS BEING DONE TO US.**

Once we understand what a "nigger" is, we will stop being afraid of a word we did not create. Once we understand that "nigger" does not define (or limit) our humanity, we will stop being ashamed of a word that *says more about the creator of the word* than it does about US.

Then, we will have the time and energy to turn our collective focus to eliminating the conditions that have created "niggers" all over the world.

"All around me I saw black men, from the sweeper to the president. As I sat in the hotel lobby and looked around, a voice in my head said to me, 'Richard, do you see black people all around you?'

To which I replied, 'Yeah, man, black all around, I have never seen so many black people in my life.'

Then the voice said, 'Richard, do you see any niggers around you?' I looked around again and said, 'No man, I don't see any niggers, only black people.'"

-- Comedian Richard Pryor speaking about a trip to the continent of Africa in 1983.

THE SINGLE MOST IMPORTANT QUESTION

#2: -- STOP Reacting And START Analyzing (What Is Being Done To And Said About Black People)

Instead of emotionally exhausting ourselves by having KNEE-JERK reactions to every racist comment that appears in the media, we have to STOP REACTING and START ANALYZING what is being said and WHY it's being said.

Once we understand that the media publicly airs racist comments to REINFORCE our *'Manufactured Black Inferiority Complex,"* **we will understand this is PROOF that we are NOT INFERIOR.**

#3: -- Limit Your Exposure To AND Support For White Supremacy "Entertainment" Programming

It is no accident that MOST TV programming degrades the images of black people. It is no accident that black males who wear or have worn dresses are the highest paid black male entertainers in the world. It is no accident that dark-skinned black females have the most degraded images in the world.

It is no accident that the most famous black actors seldom have on-screen romances with equally famous black actresses OR that black actors SELDOM romance black females in the majority of Hollywood films. It is no accident that the MAJORITY of "rap" music glorifies the degradation and murder of black people, or that these black "entertainers" are promoted as the BEST role models for black youth.

It is no accident that black males and females are shown as mutual ene-mies rather than allies in movies like *'The Color Purple, Waiting To Exhale, I Can Do Bad All By Myself, For Colored Girls, Precious, and The Blind Side* -- or that these movies often win Academy awards.

If we did not support black (and white) entertainers who degrade black people, they could not make money doing it. When our "comedy" ridicules our heroes, like Martin Luther King and Rosa Parks, our religion, churches, pastors, our beautiful black mommas, and our skin, noses, lips, and hair, WE make it harder for every black man, woman, and child to get respect at home, on the job, on the street, in the courtroom, at the mortgage company, and at the hands of law enforcement.

By supporting and defending "entertainment" that degrades black people for profit, WE are making life harder for every black male who applies for a job and is denied one because he has already been stereotyped as an irresponsible fool before he opens his mouth.

WE are making life harder for our black mothers, daughters, wives, and lovers to get the respect they deserve, when they are publicly referred to as "bitches" and "hos" by us. *If we want to win the mainstream (white) media war for our black MINDS and restore our collective sanity, we must FIGHT BACK by TUNING OUT and TAKING OUR DOLLARS WITH US.*

"I am 54 years old and I remember the luxury car commercials and the messages were always the same: buy this Cadillac, and you'll be a successful man with high status, and you'll be popular with blonde white women!

As a little boy I could never figure out why there was always a white woman with blond hair sitting in the passenger side of the car.

Naturally, when we consider that our black fathers and grandfathers watched those commercials at least ten times a day before they became grown men, we see that this "formula" for success and status was still ingrained into the black man's psyche and subconscious."

– Frank, 54, sales representative, Memphis, TN

#4: -- Stop Using The Television To Babysit Our Children

Black children are born with *an abundance of intelligence* until the media, educational system, racist whites, and unconscious black adults kill their confidence, self-esteem, and intellectual potential.

Replace television watching and video games (that do all the THINK-ING) with books, games, and building blocks, puzzles, and chemistry sets that will teach our children to THINK ANALYTICALLY and allow them to use their motor skills and creativity. If we want our children to compete intellectually with children from every part of the world, the time to prepare them is RIGHT NOW.

#5: -- Educate Yourself About The System Of White Supremacy And Our True Status In It

Until we understand WHAT white supremacy is and HOW it works, we will NOT understand what is happening to black people all over the planet. We can't create solutions until we understand the problems, the same way we can't build a house without building a foundation. What we will wind up with is a shaky, unsafe building that will topple when the first storm hits.

In the RESOURCES section, there is a list of books, CDs, DVDs, and websites that will increase your understanding of white supremacy so you will recognize HOW and WHEN it is being practiced.

#6: -- Tell Our Black Children The Truth About Racism

Jewish parents know how important it is to teach their children about the Jewish Holocaust so their children will KNOW they must be vigilant against their enemies. Two reasons so many black parents shy away from teaching our children about racism or slavery (1) out of FEAR, and (2) *we do not know enough about our history to teach anyone else.*

Once black parents AND adults understand how the system of white supremacy works, we will understand how important it is to make our children aware of WHAT is happening -- and WHY it is happening to black people all over the world.

We must STOP pretending and lying to ourselves that we should let our children "make up their own minds about race," and prepare them for the psychological attacks they will face both inside the home (TV/movies/racist video games) AND outside the home (the white supremacy system).

If we do NOT prepare them, we should be prepared -- WITHOUT COM-PLAINT) for our children to be psychologically devastated when the TRUTH AND the REALITY of racism hits them square between the eyes. It is a CRIME to let another black generation come out into a racist society without PREPARING them for what **WE KNOW** they will face in the white world.

#7: -- Let's Do The Math (Until We Know It By Heart)

SELF-VALIDATION
+
GROUP VALIDATION

= NO NEED FOR WHITE VALIDATION

NO NEED FOR WHITE VALIDATION
+
KNOWLEDGE OF SELF AND OF OUR ENEMY

= THE END OF WHITE SUPREMACY

"Afrikan parents know who they are dealing with. That's why we lie to our children in the name of protecting them. Such excuses are shameless. We are not protecting them. We are trying to protect ourselves from the pain we know will come to them and us if they stand up.

No matter how we try to play it off, we understand that Europeans will kill them in a second, for nothing. We understand that our sons are looked upon as the greatest threat to European hegemony for good reason.

And yes, as men, they are our last line of defense. There is nothing unrealistic about these fears. They are reasonable for a people who subconsciously understand the nature of their oppressor, as evidenced in historical fact, yet feel powerless to confront it.

However these reasonable fears lead to insanity when they cause us to believe that no matter what we do the European will rule forever. 'Oppression does not destroy a people. It is the acceptance of oppression that destroys."

-- "EXCUSES, EXCUSES: The Politics of Interracial Coupling in European Culture" by Mwalimu K. Baruti

Resources

Recommended Reading / Viewing

BOOKS

Hidden Colors: The Untold History of People of Aboriginal, Moor, and African Descent by Dr. Booker T. Coleman

The Isis Papers by Dr. Frances Cress Welsing

The United-Independent Compensatory Code/System/Concept: A textbook/workbook for victims of racism (white supremacy) by Neely Fuller, Jr.

The United-Independent Compensatory Code/System/Concept: A Compensator Counter-Racist Codified Word Guide by Neely Fuller, Jr.

Enemies: The Clash of Races by Haki R. Madhubuti

Asafo: A Warrior's Guide to Manhood by Mwalimu K. Bomani Baruti

Homosexuality and the Effeminization of Afrikan Males by Mwalimu K. Bomani Baruti

Mentacide by Mwalimu K. Bomani Baruti

The New Jim Crow: Mass Incarceration in the Age of Colorblindness by Michelle Alexander

Brainwashed: Challenging the Myth of Black Inferiority by Tom Burrell

The African Origin of Civilization: Myth Or Reality by Cheikh Anta Diop

The Destruction of Black Civilization by Chancellor Williams

How Capitalism Underdeveloped Black America by Manning Marable

The Conspiracy to Destroy Black Boys by Jawanza Kunjufu

What They Never Told you in History Class by Indus Khamit-Kush

Africans at the Crossroads: African World Revolution by John Henrik Clarke

The Spook who sat by the Door by Sam Greenlee (a novel)

The Golden Age of the Moor by Ivan Van Sertima

Your History J.A. Rogers by J.A. Rogers

The Secret Books of Egyptian Gnostics by Jean Doresse

Message to the Blackman in America by Elijah Muhhamad

Return to Glory: The Powerful Stirring of the Black Race by Joel A. Freeman, PhD, and Don B. Griffin

Black Man of the Nile and His Family by Yosef Ben-Jochannan

No Disrespect by Sister Souljah

The Psychological Covert War on Hip Hop by Professor Griff

Recommended Internet Radio & TV Shows

Gus T. Renegade and Justice
(C.O.W.S. at www.contextofwhitesupremacy.com)

Edward Williams - Counter-Racism Television Network
(www.counter-racism.com/c-r_tv/)

Recommended Websites

- www.trojanhorse1.com
- www.counter-racism.com
- www.racism-notes.blogspot.com   (Gus Renegade)
- www.justdojusticetoday.blogspot.com
- http://nonwhitealliance.wordpress.com
- www.drafrika.com   (Dr. Africa)
- www.waronthehorizon.com
- www.ebonynewschannel.blogspot.com
- www.cree7.wordpress.com
- www.thecode.net
- www.mindcontrolblackassassins.wordpress.com
- www.facebook.com/umarthepsychologist
- www.finalcall.com
- www.blackagendareport.com

Black-Owned Bookstores:

- www.azizibooks.com
- www.TWPBooks.com
- www.counter-racism.com
- www.akobenhouse.com
- www.houseofnubian.com
- www.houseofkonsciousness.com
- www.freemaninstitute.com
- www.afriware.net

AUDIO CDS

Racism & Counter Racism by Dr. Frances Cress Welsing

Maximum Development of Black Male Children by Dr. Frances C. Welsing

The Psychopathic Racial Personality by Dr. Bobby E. Wright, PhD

(above available at: www.houseofnubian.com)

No Sex Between White and Non-White People by Neely Fuller, Jr.
Racism and Counter Racism by Neely Fuller, Jr.

Racism and Counter Racism by Neely Fuller, Jr.

(available: www.counter-racism.com)

Return to Glory: The Powerful Stirring of the Black Race
by Joel A. Freeman, PhD, and Don B. Griffin

(available at www.freemaninstitute.com)

DVDS

Dr. Frances Cress Welsing on Phil Donahue Show

Dr. Frances Cress Welsing Debates Dr. William Shockley & The Analysis of The Bell Curve

The Isis Papers by Dr. Frances Cress Welsing

Racism and Mental Health by Dr. Frances Cress Welsing

Worship of the African Woman as Creator by Dr. Yosef Ben Jochannan

(above DVDs available at: www.houseofnubian.com)

A White Man's Journey Into Black History
by Joel A. Freeman, PhD

(available at www.freemaninstitute.com)

Index

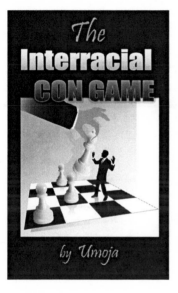

CPSIA information can be obtained at www.ICGtesting.com
Printed in the USA
BVOW03s1134290414

352036BV00001B/12/P

9 780982 206133